T WAS A MORNING LIKE ANY other, except that the perfect weather made people feel unusually energetic. The sky was a vivid blue and the sun seemed to light the tranquil water with tiny fires. As boats pulsed around the harbor, no one would have guessed that the scene was about to explode.

This was not September 11, 2001, but almost a full year earlier: October 12, 2000. The Twin Towers still stood. The Pentagon was intact. America was at peace, and the USS *Cole,* a guided missile destroyer, was making a routine refueling stop in Yemen's port of Aden.

Shortly after 11 A.M., a sailor on watch noticed a white skiff approaching the ship. The two friendly-looking men on board waved to the sailor, and he waved back. Then the little boat slammed into the *Cole,* detonating a bomb that blew a gigantic hole in the ship's side, killing 17 sailors and wounding 37.

The ship filled with acrid smoke and thousands of gallons of oily black seawater poured into the main engine room and nobody had a clue as to what was going on. It fell to the officers of the *Cole,* among them chief engineer Deborah Courtney, to make strategic choices that would keep the ship from sinking. If they failed, the *Cole* would have been the first ship to sink as a result of enemy action since World War II, more than 50 years ago.

THE USS *COLE* IS AN 8,300-TON, 505-FOOT-long, iron gray warship with a crew of 300. On that October morning the ship was two months into a six-month deployment; new recruits—men and women as young as 18—had barely gotten their sea legs. The refueling was going quickly, and many sailors had been allowed to go to lunch early, at around 11 A.M., in hopes of getting the ship under way ahead of schedule.

Just before the bomb went off, Courtney was sitting in her stateroom, in officer's country, two decks above the waterline. "The whole ship moved and we went dark," she tells me now, seven months after the attack. "Then the explosion picked me up out of my chair and dumped me on the floor." Courtney says she first believed there was a problem with the refueling. Her second thought was that something had happened with an engine. "Which," she says now, smiling ruefully,

"I found out was wrong."

Courtney knew she had to get down to CCS, the central control station, to find out where and how bad the damage was. The chief engineer is responsible for every piece of machinery on board, including the massive jet-propulsion engines and the gas turbine engines that provide electricity, and for providing power to the state-of-the-art radar panels and the advanced weaponry. Not only was Courtney in charge of all the mechanical pieces, says anti–submarine warfare officer Kyle Turner, but "she was also responsible for standing watch in combat and knowing tactically how to fight the ship in a time of war. She would be expected to make the decision to fire missiles"—vetted by the captain, of course. "Her job," Turner explains, "was to stay at Central and direct the efforts, make sure everything was calm and running in concert. If she went out and, say, actually helped shore up a bulkhead that was about to collapse, she would lose her situational awareness for the rest of the ship and her ability to make big-picture decisions."

But CCS was two decks below and aft, and the sailors running blindly through the smoke-filled passageway told her she'd never get there. So she made her way up to the bridge, where the navigator said they'd been hit by a ship. There was no sign of the small white boat the suicide bombers had used—it had been blown up in the explosion—"but you could see wet, black soot dripping everywhere," Courtney says, "and you could see, down and aft, that there was a problem on the port side of the ship. So I knew I needed to get to Central." As she rushed back down to officer's country to put on her breathing apparatus, "I went down one ladder," she says. "Kyle [Turner] went down the other. I went to CCS straight shot. He ended up in the chief's mess helping pull people out. He was a madman, just everywhere, doing whatever needed to be done."

The message couldn't be clearer. It is one I will hear again and again during my time with Deb Courtney: There was more than one hero on the *Cole.* In fact, it was a boat full of heroes. "Weren't there some people who panicked?" I ask her. She

picks up the question and turns it over, as if it's a piece of machinery to fix. "There were people who didn't show their best side," she admits. "And then there were others who in a million years you would never have thought you'd see what you saw from them." She tells me about one sailor who for 20 years had quietly done his job but who became a superhero after the bombing. "The man didn't sleep. Doc actually had to sedate him after four days. And he slept for two hours and was back up and going again."

She doesn't mention how she herself worked around the clock to prevent further flooding, which could have sunk the ship, and to forestall electrical fires—an effort requiring equal measures of skill, determination, and inventiveness. At CCS, where she met up with Lt. Comdr. Chris Peterschmidt, the *Cole*'s executive officer (XO

"THERE WERE 200 HEROES ON THAT

for short), the situation was more chaotic than she could have anticipated. Typically, engineers seated at the impressive array of electronic consoles would be able to pinpoint where damage had occurred, but that was impossible now. "That portion of the ship still had lighting," Courtney explains, "and the consoles all had power, but every single alarm on them was going off. Every light was blinking or flashing. Normally when you have an alarm, you get a line that tells you what the alarm is. But the screen was just scrolling and scrolling and scrolling." There was no way to send and receive reports over the loudspeakers. People were running into CCS, making their reports, and running out again.

Under other circumstances Courtney would have called on her senior engineers to put her damage-control plan into operation. But several of them were trapped in the chief's mess after the explosion. Senior engineer Keith Lorensen remembers that he had checked on the refueling and was finishing his lunch in the chief's mess when the bomb exploded at 11:18. "The next thing I knew, everything was silent and dark. On a navy ship, especially if you're an engineer, the last thing you want is quiet. Because that means something is bad, it means your engines aren't running." Lorensen was thrown across the room by the blast. His leg was fractured

AN OFFICER AND A GENTLE WOMAN

Almost a year before the events of September 11, terrorists bombed the USS *Cole*, killing 17 sailors. Somehow Lt. Commander Deborah Courtney managed to keep her head above water, oil, fire, smoke, and pandemonium. Cathleen Medwick reports. Photograph by Rob Howard

From left: Body cream, cologne, and shower gel, all from the Jo Malone 154 product line

AND EVERY OUNCE OF STRESS EVAPORATING.

worth buying your Clinique staples to get one of these enticing gifts—you could get a collection of skin care minis and a new shade of lipstick, or a baby-size mascara, eye shadow, and glitzy little makeup bag. Look for the Sugarplums holiday collection (glimmery makeup colors) and High Impact eye shadow duos all month.

26 **A ONE-OF-A-KIND FRAGRANCE,** made just for you, from $11. Spend an hour and a half exploring your fantasies at a custom-fragrance boutique or counter. The cost varies with the individual lines. The most notable: Aveda, $11 to $24; the new Perfumer's Palette at Nordstrom, from $30; Creed, from $400.

27 **A MANGO SUGAR GLO** at Canyon Ranch in Massachusetts's Berkshires or Tucson, Arizona, $120. This 50 minutes of exfoliating fruit massage and head-to-toe moisturizing has become the most requested treatment since its introduction at the resorts last year. If you can't get there, order the "glow to go" home spa kit, $45, stocked with Mango Sugar scrub, Mango Sugar bath & body oil, Mango Sugar body lotion, and mango-scented candles (call 800-726-8040 to order products).

28 **TRIPLE-MILLED, OVERSIZE BATH SOAP—** for the creamy, blanketlike lather and the sensory thrill of running a giant bar over your skin. Two of the very best: Yves Saint Laurent Nu, $25 (a black soap that produces frothy white suds), and Baudelaire Provence Santé honeysuckle body bar, $15 (which is so beautiful, you almost hate to get it wet).

29 **ORIGINS TWO-WAY-STRETCH MULTI-HAND MASSAGE,** $150, is as delightful as it sounds. Two pairs of professionally trained hands plus your tired body equals an unforgettable 50 minutes. Available exclusively at Origins Feel Good Spa at Chelsea Piers in New York City.

30 **A FRAGRANCE WARDROBE** from Jo Malone. The British perfumer is taking her signature scent public. Jo Malone 154, the exquisite blend of grapefruit, herbs, and musk worn by the perfume mistress herself for years, is now available as a cologne, $45, body cream, $75, and shower gel, $35.

31 **A JOURNEY TO BEGAWAN GIRI ESTATE IN BALI,** Indonesia, a place so private you might feel it's your own estate. Experience sybaritic pleasures like a Taksu or Balinese massage or a hibiscus and aloe vera body treatment in a spectacular setting that includes emerald tropical gardens, a semicircular infinity pool, and private meditation gardens (www.begawan.com).

32 **AVEDA LIP TINTS** in Peony and Spice, $11 each. The quintessential no-makeup makeup, and an upgrade from basic balm, adds just a hint of color so you can apply it without a mirror. Put one of these in your purse and keep it there. Everyday use guaranteed.

33 **A BIG, PLUSH BATH SHEET** from Banana Republic, $36, makes drying yourself off as sensuous as the soak that comes before.

34 **ONE MONTH WITH A PERSONAL TRAINER.** It can cost as little as $80 and go up to around $2,000. Nothing provides better motivation for a workout than hiring—and paying for—your very own drill sergeant.

35 **LAURA MERCIER HONEY BATH** in Crème Brûlée, $40. Use the accompanying wooden honey dipper to drop a dollop of this creamy gelée into running water and let the fragrance fill the room. Lock the door, slip into the bath, and don't come out for a good, long time. ●
For details see Shop Guide.

Lt. Commander
Deborah Courtney
at the Norfolk
Naval Station in
Virginia seven
months after the
bombing of her
ship in Yemen

Palaces of Florence

Francesco Gurrieri
Patrizia Fabbri

Palaces of Florence

Photography
Stefano Giraldi

RIZZOLI
NEW YORK

Photo credits:
p. 96, left: Archivio Scala, Florence
pp. 42, 44–49: Raffaello Bencini

First published in the United States of America in 1996 by
Rizzoli International Publications, Inc.
300 Park Avenue South, New York, NY 10010

First published in Italy in 1995 by
Arsenale Editrice srl
San Polo 1789
I-30125 Venezia

Library of Congress Cataloging-in-Publication Data

Gurrieri, Francesco.
[Palazzi di Firenze. English]
    Palaces of Florence / Francesco Gurrieri, Patrizia Fabbri;
photography by Stefano Giraldi.
        p.   cm.
    Includes bibliographical references and index.
    ISBN 0-8478-1965-5 (hc)
    1. Palaces—Italy—Florence.   2. Florence (Italy)—Buildings,
structures, etc. I. Fabbri, Patrizia. II. Title.
NA7755.G8613 1996
28.8'2'094551—dc20   96-18491
                                                CIP

Printed in Italy

Table of Contents

Introduction

The historic, artistic, and architectural heritage of every nation is an essential part of its cultural identity. Unless we wish to lose our memory of the past, it is necessary to hand down culture and traditions to future generations. One way of doing this is through the preservation of historic buildings and gardens, by warding off deterioration and destruction.

Historic homes are not always museums. Preserving them in some cases means allowing them to be used actively, or living in them. We cannot encase them in amber, but we can find uses that are compatible with the purposes for which they were originally built.

With this purpose, the Associazione Dimore Storiche Italiane was founded in 1977, in emulation of similar associations in other European countries. The purpose of the association is to work toward the conservation of the nation's architectural heritage; it is believed that this will contribute to the overall preservation of our cultural heritage, in the best public interest. Knowledge is the fundamental stake in any work of preservation, hence the interest of the Associazione Dimore Storiche Italiane in promoting projects for the study, exploration, and popularization of our architectural heritage. This book is working in precisely the areas that our association roundly encourages, and constitutes a major auxiliary tool for architectural preservation.

All of the private owners of the Florentine palazzi described in this volume are members of our association. They contribute in a decisive manner to preserving Florence's aspect as a city of splendid monumental buildings. For some of these owners, the commitment to preservation dates from the earliest times, down the family tree; it was their forefathers who first built the palazzi that still occupy a central place in city life. Let us extend our appreciation, and that of the authors, to them.

Niccolò Rosselli Del Turco
Vice President of the Associazione Dimore Storiche Italiane
(Association for Historic Homes of Italy)

Preface

One of the reasons we three authors have produced this book is our desire to go beyond the outmoded, static concept of architecture, whereby a building is an entity that is historically, architecturally, and stylistically complete on the day construction ends for the first time, a single unit with an intrinsic value and meaning, rendering the building immune to the shifts and mutations of time and history. This approach can be acceptable, of course, but only if it is based upon criteria of precision that are fundamental to an adequate exploration of urban history and present reality.

Behind the centuries-old facades of the palazzi, however—facades that are not always unchangeable or unchanged—in the intimacy of family life, lives and history have rolled on in silence. We have decided to take a respectful look at what has gone on behind this curtain of silence. Hence, we have examined carefully the interiors, the furnishings, and the gardens, at whose existence those walking by in the street would never even guess. Hence the intentionally vivid and original style of the photography, which is not only a documentary substratum of historical and architectural description, but is itself a description. In certain cases, we encountered predictable obstacles that were part and parcel of this approach—when our work was greeted as an unwarranted intrusion into family privacy, as an interruption in the busy working week of a bank or public office, or as a premature "scoop" on a campaign of restoration—aspects of the natural defense of privacy that did little if anything to compromise the completeness of this volume.

And this gives us one more reason to extend our sincere and heartfelt thanks to all those—private citizens, companies, and banks—who, with their courtesy, their generous helpfulness, and even with their sensitivity, have made this project possible in their awareness of their exceptional roles as trustees and custodians of an ancient tradition.

Lastly, in particular, we would like to thank Rodolfo Budini Gattai for his invaluable collaboration; also we would like to thank Giulio Barbolani di Montauto, Guido Ciompi, Dora Manetti, Daniele Nepi, and Pietro Ruschi.

Francesco Gurrieri, Patrizia Fabbri, Stefano Giraldi

The Florentine Palazzo: Stability, comfort, beauty

Francesco Gurrieri

Florence in 1352: detail of the
fresco in the Sala del Consiglio in
the Bigallo.

As recently as 1905, when Janet Ross published *Florentine Palaces and Their Stories* (J.M. Dent & Co., London), very little had appeared concerning the palazzi of Florence. What did exist was, by and large, limited to architectural descriptions that rarely, if ever, included observations concerning the interiors, the gardens, and the furnishings. The existing literature could rely on nothing more systematic than the much-esteemed compendium by E. Mazzanti-Del Lungo (*Raccolta delle migliori fabbriche antiche e moderne in Firenze*, Florence, 1876).

During roughly the same years, Carl von Stegmann and Heinrich von Geymüller published their work *Die Architektur der Renaissance in Toskana* (Munich, 1890–1906); in it they described a number of Florentine palazzi. Still, for the most part, this field remained quite sketchy and anything but systematic for some time to come. It was not until 1910 that the most complete known inventory of architecture and urban spaces (featuring an essential basic bibliography) was published: Walther Limburger's *Die Gebäude von Florenz, Architekten, Strasse und Plätze in alphabetischen Verzeichnissen* (Leipzig).

A view of Santa Maria del Fiore, taken from the ramparts of the Forte di Belvedere. Note the dramatic thrust of the Torre di Arnolfo.

St. Zanobi holds up Florence (detail), school of Perugino, church of San Martino Strada, Grassina. Zanobi was a particularly venerated bishop of Florence, and became one of the city's patron saints.

A series of monographic contributions on individual palazzi followed, many of them exploring the subject in great depth; in particular, we should cite those by Giuseppe Poggi, Giuseppe Marchini, Piero Sanpaolesi, and Günther and Christel Thiem. At last, the exceedingly useful and systematic work by Leonardo Ginori Lisci was published (*I palazzi di Firenze nella storia e nell'arte*, Florence, 1972, 2 volumes). It followed hard on the heels of an equally laudable effort by Bucci and Benicini (*Palazzi di Firenze*, Florence, 1971). The years that followed saw the publication of further monographic studies on Palazzo Medici Riccardi, Palazzo Tornabuoni, and Palazzo Strozzi (this last effort was particularly noteworthy for its approach and its sagacious coordination of expertise; it was edited by Daniela Lamberini).

At this point in our account, however, we should stop for a moment to reflect upon an exquisitely methodological consideration: the historical analysis of the palazzi of Florence has been distinctly shaped by the historiography of the past, as well as by the personalities of the various authors. That may seem like an obvious statement, or even a tautology, and yet it is worthy of exploration. Only recently, in fact, has our reading, or analysis of the Florentine palazzo been enriched, synchronically, with the various other components that so greatly contributed to its

overall image, its general cultural, social, and economic significance. What existed was a body of thorough and learned analysis of the facades, the architectural styles, and the sculptural and pictorial accompaniments to the main architectural theme. The history of the individual families has been progressively fleshed out with an economic, or material history (thoroughly and rigorously documented), so that it is finally possible to understand a palazzo in its progressive development, in the motivations that underlie it, in the meaning and roles of the human relationships that were played out within it, and in the more complex story of courtly life and the relationships that marked the mercantile middle class, such a major factor in the history of Florence. It took a few tentative studies of the furnishings of the Florentine home, followed by others on Florentine society and secret treasures, to carve out the bed of a new stream of historiography; this new branch of study proved in time to be of considerable importance. Then there were exquisite archival studies that offered objective information on the construction of the palazzi; a fine example of this body of work are the studies by Guido Pampaloni on Palazzo Salviati, Palazzo Datini (in Prato), and Palazzo Strozzi. These archival studies triggered a chain reaction of other, more complex studies.

For the interiors of the palazzi, a decisive role was

played by an exhibition—the *Mostra dei Tesori Segreti delle Case Fiorentine*, (Exhibition of the Secret Treasures of the Houses of Florence)—curated by Mina Gregori, with the assistance of Mina Bacci and Carlo Donzelli. The exhibition comprised no fewer than 335 objects, including paintings and objects of furniture, and clearly showed just how important the furnishing was to the building as a whole.

We should also make note of the great cultural effort involved in the organization of a handsome exhibition held in 1966 (accompanied by highly useful catalogs). This exhibition was entitled *Firenze ai Tempi di Dante* (Florence in the Time of Dante); it was held at the Certosa del Galluzzo, a charterhouse, and was curated by Raffaello Ramat. The occasion was the seventh centennial of the birth of Dante Alighieri.

During this same period, Federigo Melis was completing his monumental efforts to reorganize the archives of Casa Datini in Prato; his work provided a cross-section image of the economic and social life of a merchant who was already more European than merely Florentine, a merchant who traded throughout the Mediterranean basin and in much of modern Europe.

The restoration of Casa Datini (by Nello Bemporad) and the reorganization of the Datini archives set a major precedent and constituted an important opportunity to encourage the study of inter-

national economic history. And, in this context, the history of the palazzi of Florence developed.

Last but certainly not least came various studies by Richard A. Goldthwaite ("The Florentine Palace as Domestic Architecture," in *American Historical Review*, LXXVII, 1972; and *The Building of Renaissance Florence*, London, 1980); and studies by Christiane Klapish on family life, by F. W. Kent on the relations between politics and the home, and by Kent Lydecker on furniture and furnishings.

Clearly, there was a groundswell of interest, based on previous studies (Elio Conti, Federigo Melis, Guido Pampaloni), rendering more complex and more syncretic the foundations of that school of historiography.

Monte di Giovanni, *St. Zanobi*, mosaic, Opera del Duomo di Firenze. In the background, note the view of fortified Florence.

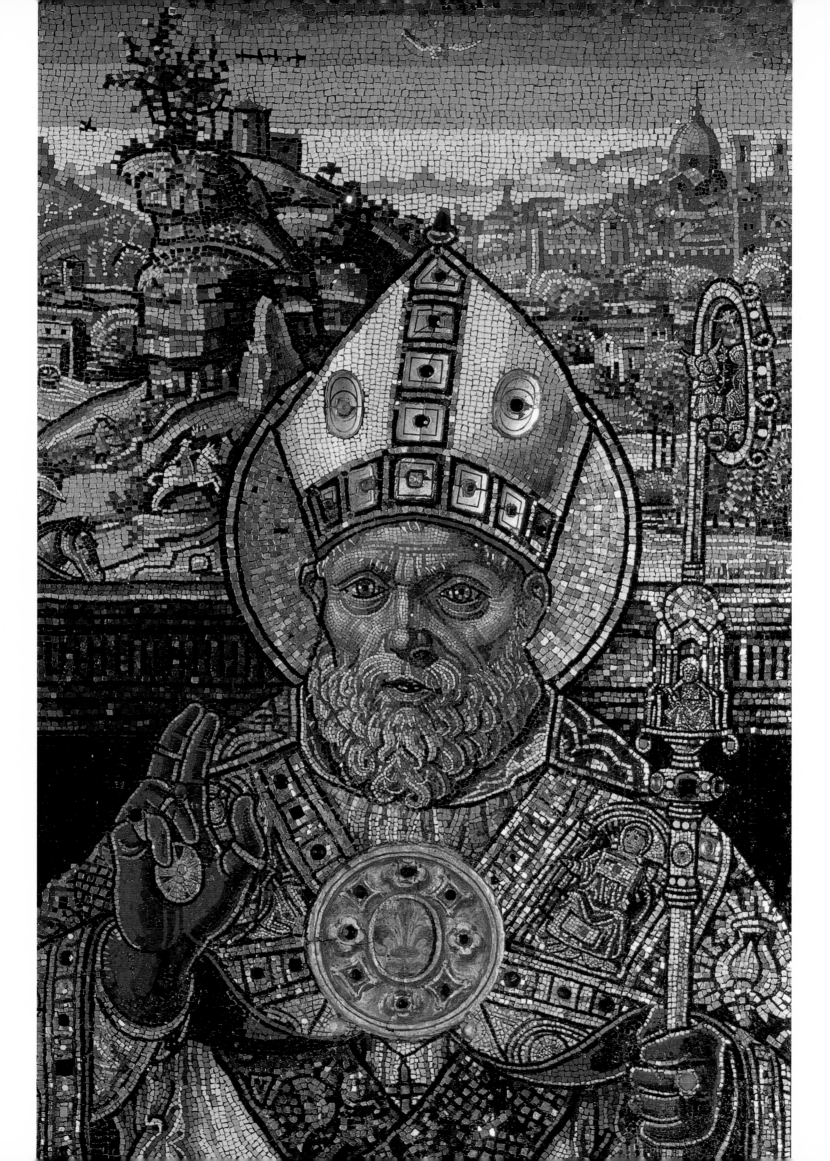

From the tower-house to the fortified palazzo

And so it becomes fundamental to provide a critical reexamination of the development of these ideas, ideas which had already been guessed at and hinted at in studies of architecture and restoration.

This body of thought developed through the work of scholars (among them Gustavo Giovannoni, Luigi Crema, Piero Sanpaolesi, and, later on, Eugenio Battisti) who approached their architectural studies from a point of view beyond mere formal analysis. For them, to speak of a palazzo meant speaking of its materiality, of the fact that it was made up of typological parts (walls, windows, roofs, attics, floors, doors, stairs, decorations, and various facilities), each of which had its own specific use and purpose.

If we wish to speak of the Florentine palazzo, then, we must establish the parameters of the transition within which the term palazzo is adequately specific and clearly recognizable. We may then range freely from the transition of the medieval residence into the home of the early Renaissance, from the late tower-house to the European-style palazzo found in the great eighteenth-century period that sowed the seeds of neoclassicism, abandoning the last delightful glimmers of *barocchetto*, or late baroque.

The first transition began with the remarkable typology of the tower-house, which had been a dominant fixture in the landscape of the medieval, and even the Renaissance town.

Just what were these symbols of power, these tools of attack and defense that the most powerful families built alongside their homes? What were these buildings that, during the years of factional strife, so altered the face of Florence? Just how did these full-fledged instruments of military strategy work, disguised as they were by fanciful and enchanting nicknames—the "Begazza" of the Cassigiani family; the "Galganetta" of the Nerli family, later owned by the Machiavelli family; the "Rognosa" in Porta Rossa. In some cases, the towers were given the names of the family itself, such as the splendid Torri degli Amidei on Por Santa Maria, the Torre dei Consorti near the Ponte Vecchio, and the Torre dei Marsili in Borgo San Jacopo.

In later years, many of these towers were *appalagiate*, or incorporated into palazzi; in some cases they were used as the structural foundations of bell towers (for example, the campanile of Santa Felicita), which meant that they shared the fate of many other towers outside of the city walls, which were used as bell towers for so many country parish churches.

Florence in 1352: detail of the fresco in the Sala del Consiglio in the Bigallo, which depicts the *Madonna della Misericordia* (Our Lady of Mercy).

The construction and location of these towers was anything but unregulated, as so many scholars seem to think. The function of the modern zoning and planning commissions and the civil engineers was back then the jurisdiction of the Ufiziali di Torre (Tower Officials). It is still possible to see their stone escutcheon depicting a crenelated tower on the Ponte Vecchio, just beneath the Loggia del Grano, and elsewhere in Florence. They were colleagues of the Ufiziali in charge of streets, bridges, and walls. The entire field of construction was thus regulated. *Materia edificatoria* was the term of the period; construction and urban planning might be the modern equivalent.

The Ufiziali delle Cinque Cose (Officials of the Five Things) as they were later called, were responsible for the construction of bridges and watermills, the clearing and broadening of streets and squares, the establishment of official distances, and the restoration of public buildings and walls (with the authorization of the Gonfaloniere and the Priori, high city officials).

Just like the towers, the tower-houses were residences that occupied very little surface area: each side of a tower-house usually extended only ten or twelve *braccia*, the equivalent of six to seven meters. Thus the area occupied on the ground was never more than about twenty-five square meters (the size of a modern living room). The

arrangement of the interior was exceedingly simple, so that the personalization of a tower-house was primarily a matter of furnishings.

Florence, Rome, Bologna, Lucca, Pisa, Pistoia, Prato, Pavia, Volterra, and San Gimignano were among the most turreted cities in Italy. Scholars such as C. Lupi, who have thoroughly studied the problems of the medieval house in various archives, have made it possible for us to verify and understand the iconographic information that survives from pictorial narratives of the fourteenth and fifteenth centuries. We can thus better grasp the meaning of certain images painted by Giotto, the architectural backgrounds Masaccio painted in the Brancacci Chapel, scenes in the *Metaphor of Good Government* in the Palazzo Pubblico in Siena, in the *Madonna della Misericordia* fresco in the Bigallo, and, really, in the entire body of late-medieval urban iconography.

This typology of the tower-house persisted as late as the early Renaissance, and spread far beyond the geographic boundaries of central Italy. Palazzo Davanzati is a good example of the survival of the tower-house in one of the loveliest and most impressive of fourteenth-century buildings. In Viterbo, the Palazzo degli Alessandri (thirteenth century) has a facade that still features some singular elements: the windows with cross arches, and a large balcony beneath a huge basket

The poor expelled from Siena find shelter in Florence: a celebrated miniature from the Biadaiolo Codex, fourteenth century.

The Catena plan of Florence (detail), fifteenth century.

ORTO S' MICHELE
S. CROCE
RICASOLESI
PONTE ALLA KARRAIA
PONTEASTRINITA

arch that spans nearly the entire facade.

The tower-house was truly quite simple in structure. Two solid stone pillars (rarely, three or four) were linked at the top of the building by pointed or round arches. The intermediate floors were punctuated by stone or wooden architraves, or by hollow brick arches. Upon them rested wooden floors and platforms. The *tours gigantesques qui s'élévaient jusqu'aux nues* (giant towers, reaching up to the clouds) as Rouhault de Fleury described them in an account of his travels through Tuscany in the nineteenth century, were located in the *area plana* within the city walls. The roofs had a pavilion or shed structure; made of wood, they terminated in sharply projecting eaves. The eaves, visible from the street, served not only as protection for the facade and to shelter passers-by from rain; they almost invariably served as emblems of pride, even ostentation, for the family that built or owned a palazzo. The sharply projecting eaves were supported not only by brackets—simple or compound, with various sorts of sub-brackets—but also by small beams, properly braced at an angle to support the weight and strain of the eaves. The ceilings were also made of wood (the term *palco* was used to indicate the lower surface of a story, i.e., the floor; while *solaio* was used to indicate the upper surface of a story, i.e., the ceiling) and were used to define the various rooms. The

solai did not necessarily cover the entire area of the building. In some cases they covered only a section; thus, there developed *solai mozzi*, or truncated ceilings, which the Pisans called *solaiuoli*. The Florentines called them *mezzanini*. In some cases, two rooms on the same floor were linked by *ballatoi*, or balconies made of wood and jutting from the walls on underpinnings made of stone brackets or corbels. Connecting the balconies and the ceiling/floors, one with another, were stairways in stone or wood. In some cases elegant windows were added. These tended to be twin-light mullioned windows, with large, centered arches bisected by a slender central column supporting two small round arches. Three-light and four-light mullioned windows were used as well (in Palazzo Astai in Pisa, for instance).

On the ground floor, for the most part, was the *bottega* or *fondaco*, a combination workshop and storage area. On the upper stories, connected by wooden stairways, were a number of rooms, very similar to one another, used for domestic tasks and for sleeping. The tower-house was generally inhabited as follows: the piano nobile, or main floor, usually the second story, held the living quarters of the lord himself. The higher stories held the living quarters of the family. Servants and subjects were distributed in huts and hovels, either built on the higher stories, or clustered around the tower-house. This distribution

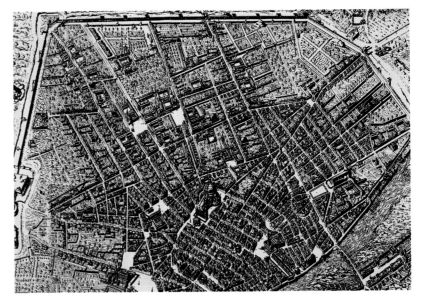

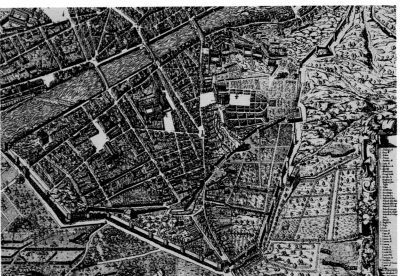

Details of the plan of Florence by Fra Stefano Bonsignori (sixteenth century), which show how dense and far-reaching the city structure had already become.

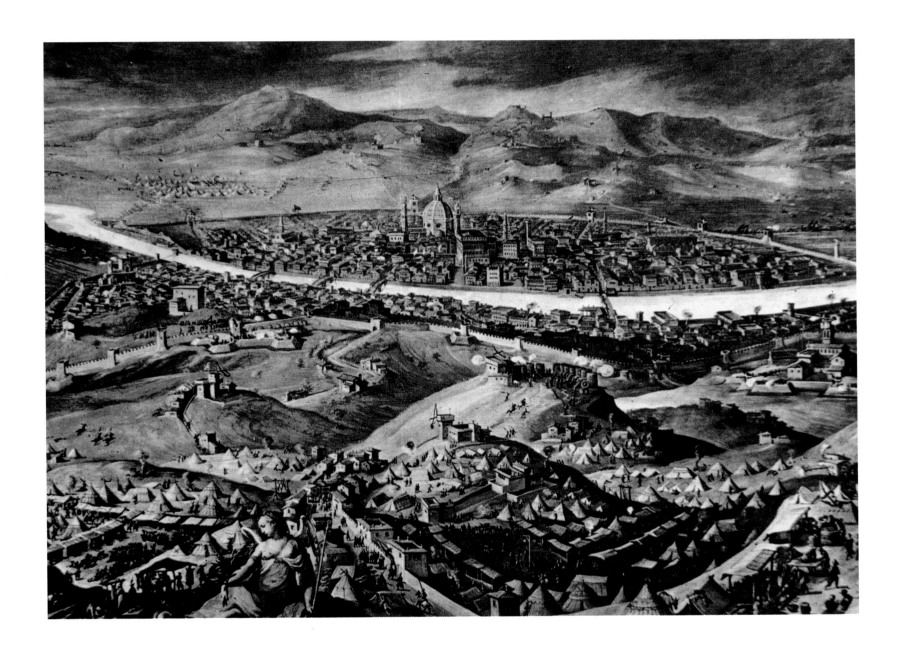

Giorgio Vasari, *The Siege of
Florence in 1530,* Sala di Clemente
VII, Palazzo Vecchio.

of living quarters was found in Florentine tower-houses, just as it is found in the buildings on Via delle Belle Torri in Pisa; in Lucca on Via Fillungo and Via Santa Lucia, in Prato on Via Pugliesi and Piazza Santa Maria in Castello, in Pistoia in the Case di Catilina, or the recently discovered houses on Via Puccini.

The preference was to locate the kitchen as high as possible, in order to make smoke ventilation less of a problem, and to prevent the chimney from running through the entire height of the building, which would have posed a serious fire danger. The hygienic facilities consisted of the sink (known as the *acquaiolo* in the fourteenth century); this structure was often built into a wall niche, in masonry, with runoff pipes that in some cases emptied into the town sewers—where such things as sewers existed—or else directly into the public street through a hole in the wall with a projecting spout. As a result of the law against outdoor latrines, these were placed in points that were accessible to all, often quite near the kitchen. The runoff pipes from the latrines—often flowing confluently with rainwater drainage from the roof—emptied into channels beneath the houses, with consequences for neighboring houses that can easily be imagined.

As for the materials employed, the Florentines used stone and terra-cotta (*tegole* (curved roofing tiles); *embrici* (flat tiles); *tavelle* (hol-low flat tiles); *tomboli* (round tile pipes); *culminali* (summit tiles); and *embricioni* (particularly large, flat tiles). The Florentines also used lime mortar and stone slabs (*ardesia* and *lavagna*, two types of slate), lumber of all sorts (chestnut, durmast oak, pine, and elm). They used iron, and in some cases lead.

Having described the layout of the various rooms of the house, let us now examine the furnishings. Benches and chests, decorated and carved, were common items of furniture; people received visitors in their bedrooms, so next to the bed stood cupboards, strongboxes, coffers, and painted headboards, in all shapes and sizes, as well as tapestries with Saracen designs in the Eastern style. It was quite rare to have glazed windows (only the wealthiest enjoyed the luxury of glass); it was far more common to cover windows openings with pieces of oiled or waxed cloth, or else with wooden shutters.

The tower-house appears to us now as the protagonist of a hard-won civil and political equilibrium that was complex and volatile; in it we can glimpse a microcosm of the city of Florence, with its traditions and perennial contradictions. As alluring as the idea of the tower-studded city, set within its walled perimeter, may be, it comprises other harsh aspects of reality as well, such as those that emerge from the portrait that Leonardo Bruni offers us: "A number of cities are so unclean that whatever filth is produced during the night appears before the eyes of the people the next morning, to be trodden underfoot; it is impossible to imagine anything filthier. Indeed, though the populace might be in the millions, and though there might be inexhaustible wealth and a limitless multitude of

Valerio Spada, *View of Florence*, seventeenth century (property of the Cassa di Risparmio di Firenze).

people, all the same, I would roundly condemn so unclean a city, and would never hold it in high esteem . . ." (*Laudatio Florintinae Urbis*, 1403)

It is further evident that nearly everything we have said of the tower-house was also true of the Renaissance palazzo. Indeed, we can summarize, as follows, the features that constituted substantial new developments:

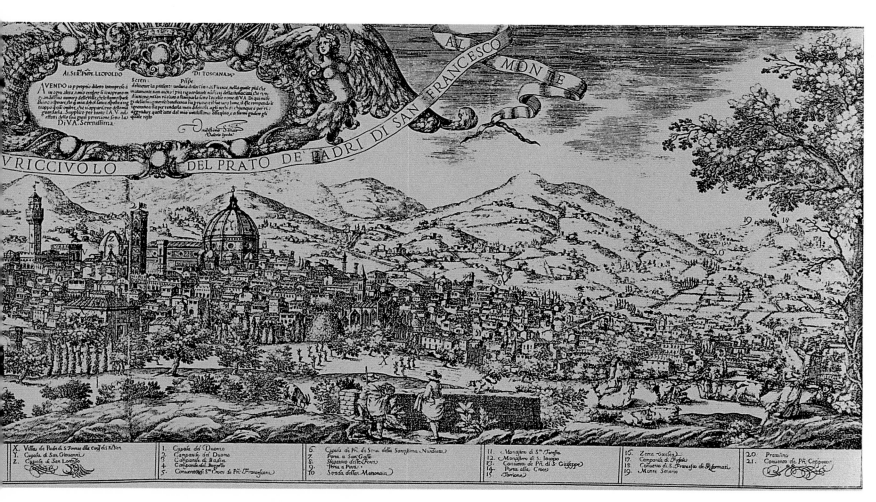

The Santissima Annunziata, the
convent complex of the Servites,
and Palazzo Budini Gattai, with its
unfinished section (seventeenth
century).

—A different layout of the rooms, or halls, which now became distinctive and ennobling features of the palazzo as a whole. The staircase was now built with each step carved from a single piece of stone. The handrail was built into the walls at a proper height to offer a grip to those descending or climbing the stairs. The stairwell was generally covered with a barrel-vault ceiling, with the curving ceiling structure supported on a running stone cornice. Where stairwell vaults met at the landings, they were connected by cross vaults, necessarily supported by stone corbels. Stone carvers tended to unleash all of their creativity and skill on these corbels, though generally in accordance with the design of the chief architect. The steps themselves were no longer square-hewn, with sharp corners. Now they were finished with a circular fillet, which came to form a useful projection between the riser and the step, so that the foot was accommodated more securely.

—A greater and more systematic use of a vaulted system; the flat, wooden ceilings were replaced with large barrel or groin vaults. The spandrel points of the groin vaults were used to join the ceiling structure with the oblique embrasures of the windows. These allowed light to enter, and permitted the window shutters to be opened. The vaults were set on stone brackets or corbels; upon these were engraved the insignia or monograms of the family, especially in reception halls used for entertainment.

—The eaves of the roof now tended to project considerably. There seemed to be a competition to build eaves with the greatest extension. These eaves were made variously of stone (as in Palazzo

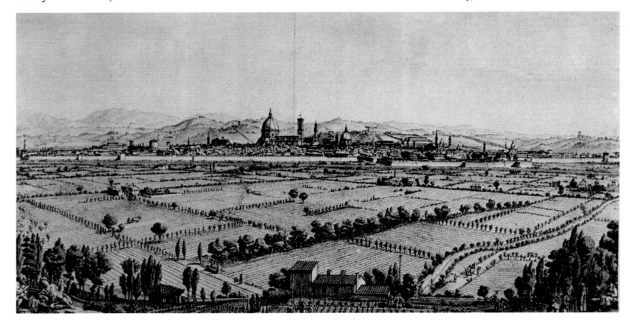

View of Florence from the Convent of the Cappuccini di Montughi (Giuseppe Zocchi, eighteenth century).

Strozzi) or wood (Palazzo Corsini Suarez on Via Maggio); in the panels between the brackets we see elaborate rosettes, as well as heraldic crests or family insignia. The extent of the projection—especially when the eaves were made of stone—created new problems of static engineering in the roof structure and the top stories of the building, obliging interior load-bearing structures to provide equilibrium for the structure as a whole, against the considerable overbalance. One typical case is the large cornice of Palazzo Strozzi, one of the most daring constructions of the entire Renaissance; built in ashlars

The Bargello, with Palazzo Nonfinito in the background (Giuseppe Zocchi, eighteenth century).

View of Piazzetta Antinori, with Palazzo Antinori in the background (Giuseppe Zocchi, eighteenth century).

The Piazza di Santa Trinita, with Palazzo Feroni and Palazzo Bartolini Salimbeni (Giuseppe Zocchi, eighteenth century).

Bottom The amphitheater of Palazzo Pitti in an eighteenth-century print.

of *pietra forte* (coarse stone), the structure juts inward as well (in a sort of balancing effect) with dovetailed toothing, both vertically and horizontally.

—Inside the buildings, the walls were systematically covered with strictly lime-based plaster, applied with a hand trowel, to create a slightly uneven surface that was pleasing to the eye. The doors were clearly marked with architraves, friezes, and stone jambs, upon which one could read the family monogram or crest. The stairwell was always present, and ran through the height of the various stories, with feeder windows at every floor. The various moldings employed were so clearly defined in stylistic terms that they can be used not only to date the construction, but even to establish the identity of the architect.

Interiors and exteriors

When the *Vocabolario degli Accademici della Crusca*, the Italian equivalent of the Oxford English Dictionary, first appeared in 1612, the term *palazzo* (or *Palagio*, as it was written), was defined as an isolated home, or, commonly, any large residential structure (generally having a large courtyard). Still, the syntactic use of the term palazzo traces its roots back to the transitional house that existed between the fourteenth and fifteenth century. The following is a summary and extracts from the chapter

concerning the *casa* found in the catalogue from the show *Firenze ai Tempi di Dante*.

Near the *sala madornale*, or great hall, stood the kitchen; in both rooms there were large fireplaces, obviously serving radically different functions; one was used to cook food, the other was a

primary source of heat. In each room there invariably stood a water basin or sink. The one in the *sala madornale* was used for washing one's hands before and after meals, and tended to be refined in appearance. It comprised a basin called the *tinocolo*, and a water container that was hidden in the wall.

"Every morning—says Ser Paolo—when you rise, wash your hands and your face before leaving your house; likewise when you sit down for a meal, be it dinner, lunch, or breakfast, always wash your hands. Likewise, when you get up from the table, after dinner, lunch, or breakfast, wash your hands and your mouth and teeth,

and you will be clean: it is an admirable custom." (Giovanni Villani, *Storia di Giovanni Villani cittadino fiorentino*, 1587)

Standing beside the sink were wooden shelves, often built into the wall, on which glasses, pitchers, and other such utensils were stored; from the wall hung towels upon which one could dry one's hands. The floors were usually made of terra-cotta tiles, arranged in various ways, or glazed terra-cotta, or—in some exceedingly rare cases—marble inlay.

The *sala madornale* was decorated with benches and chests; the chests were sometimes embellished with painted scenes or with carvings of various subjects. The chests were particularly common because every bride who entered the house of her new husband came bearing one or two chests containing her trousseau. The benches, which were quite simple in structure, were made more comfortable for guests by covering them with brightly

Thomas Patch, *View of Florence*, 1776 (property of the Cassa di Risparmio di Firenze).

Caspar Van Wittel, *Florence seen from the Mulina di San Niccolò,* eighteenth century (property of the Cassa di Risparmio di Firenze).

colored blankets known as *pancali*.

The few tables that existed were likewise quite simple in structure, consisting of a platform made of cypress boards on unadorned legs, and were not a permanent part of the furnishing. Tables were used only during meals, and when the meal was finished, they were broken down and put away.

Chairs tended to be prized items of furniture, and were not common at all. Often, each chair had a small accompanying folding table, which could be carried from one room to another.

The utensils used at table were roughly those we use today—spoon, knife, and fork; the fork dates from the late thirteenth century, and became common in the fourteenth century. The material and the form of these utensils varied according to one's economic resources. Suffice it to say that spoons, forks, and knives were even made out of rock crystal, silver, and gold. The ivory or wooden handles of knives were often finely adorned and worked. Dishes, bowls, glasses, and pitchers were generally made out of terra-cotta, but some soon replaced them with wrought silver, in some cases enameled wrought silver.

The bedroom often served as a reception area as well; there one would spend time with friends or even hold official meetings or audiences. Pope Boniface VIII, in 1300, received the ambassadors of a number of cities, including the Florentine ambassadors, sitting in his bedroom.

Besides the bed, the other items of furniture were those commonly found in fourteenth-century homes: strongboxes, cupboards, a *suppedano* or a *scrigno* (specific types of coffers or strongboxes), chests in which to store clothing, linen, and other valuable objects. The bed might have a number of shapes, but it was generally surrounded by a curtain, usually made of precious materials, such as silks or German fabrics. In that case, the bed was known as a *camera*, or chamber, because the "baladchin" gave it a room-like configuration. The most refined blankets or covers tended to be made of silk, or of French fabrics with appliqué decorations. Beds might have a wooden decoration in place of a simple headboard.

There were few items of household furniture, and those that existed were quite simple in form. Sets of very specific regulations governed all Arti (Guilds) concerned; these regulations strictly prescribed how furniture could be made, establishing proper sizes, the types of wood to be used, even methods of construction.

As early as the fourteenth century, it had become common practice to hang wooden panels with religious paintings in various rooms. Painted wooden statues, depicting the Virgin Mary especially, were considered part of the furnishings, even if they—like the wooden panels just mentioned—were also objects of veneration. The furnishing of fourteenth-century houses might also be enriched by upholstery or wall hangings used to adorn rooms on such occasions as weddings. On those occasions, the walls were decked with draperies, known as *capoletti*, literally "heads of beds," as in bedsteads, as Giovanni Villani indicates in one passage, when he says that a "courtyard was decked with very fine French *capoletti*."

The name *capoletti* comes from their original use, when they were employed in place of headboards. They might be made of silk, or more commonly, of French serge; they were often painted, and the painters who did this work were known as *sargiali*. Other draperies—also decorated with aristocratic escutcheons, plant motifs, and geometric designs—also covered benches, while others still hung from the walls over the benches as backrests.

The Crusades had made it common practice to own Eastern carpets, especially wool carpets. In later years, the most successful manufacturers of these household products were in France; there they were known as *tapis sarrassinois*, i.e., Saracen carpets, imitations of Eastern originals right down to the patterns. In Florence, these rugs were imported from France, and they were chiefly used to cover articles of furniture such as strongboxes and beds.

When the museum show, *Tesori Segreti delle Case Fiorentine*

Giovanni Signorini, *View of the Ponte Vecchio, looking toward the Ponte alle Grazie,* 1884 (property of the Cassa di Risparmio di Firenze).

(Secret Treasures of the Houses of Florence) opened, it was easy to see that the treasuries were largely composed of ". . . paintings by masters, sculptures that seemed almost to breathe, pieces of furniture that had been caressed by the light hands of time, refined and powerful bronzes, admirably chased silverwork, remarkable majolica that still throbbed with the cunning flames of the craftsman's kiln, princely porcelain tableware, stout iron armor, well-worn carpets whose weave still preserves the miraculous colors of another age, rare volumes whose gilt lettering seems to tell of a fabled world, ivories, fabrics, enamels, and jade . . ." (Giorgio Batini, *Mostra dei tesori segreti delle case fiorentine*, 1960)

The stones of Florence

We should also point out that the materials used in building walls and, more particularly, facades in Florence tended to comprise two types of stone, quarried in the area around Florence:
—*pietra forte*, a "strong," coarse stone that was used quite extensively in the Middle Ages, continued to be used for the larger buildings (Palazzo Pitti, Palazzo Strozzi, Palazzo Medici, Palazzo Antinori);
—*pietra serena*, a "gentle," finer stone popularized especially by Brunelleschi; this stone in time was used in refined moldings, capitals, corbels, and friezes.

The first scholar to study the use of these two stone materials in a systematic manner was Francesco Rodolico, in his fundamental work, *Le Pietre delle Città d'Italia* (Florence, 1953, 1964, 1995).

Rodolico wrote: "The fortified palazzi of the Renaissance represent a further

development of Florentine medieval architecture; they are clearly distinguished by rustication utilizing *pietra forte* ashlars; these are the 'stupendous buildings made of ashlars' that Vasari so admired, 'like that of Casa Medici, the facade of Palazzo Pitti, Palazzo Strozzi, and countless others.' And Vasari added: 'For this sort of building, the more solid and simple [the ashlars] are, and the better the design, the more artistry and beauty is found within; it is necessary that this sort of building be longer-lasting and more eternal than other

buildings; therefore larger blocks of stone are used, and they are better joined; the building is assembled with one stone joined to another. And because the stones are properly hewn and solid, misfortune and the passage of time are powerless to harm the building, so well do they

carve and perforate the stones, hanging them, as Florentines say, in mid-air.' The gradated ashlar-work, or rustication, of Palazzo Strozzi is particularly vigorous, as is that of Palazzo Pitti. The latter is entirely composed of stone that was quarried right on the spot, on the Boboli hill directly behind the palazzo (in fact, Palazzo Pitti was built on the site of a quarry). There is an undefinable sense of the picturesque about Palazzo Medici, conferred by the various styles of *pietra forte*. The ground floor is constructed of rusticated ashlars,

followed by flat ashlars on the second floor and seamless ashlars on the top floor [see illustration, page 51]. And in the facades, there is an occasional ashlar that stands out for its unusual size (not height, for the most part, but length: some of them range from [thirteen to twenty-six feet]).

"Rather than concentrate on the ashlars that make up the bottom section of Palazzo Pitti, let us consider the enormous ashlar that was hoisted up over the portal of Palazzo Strozzi that overlooks Via de' Tornabuoni: the workers that hauled it and set it into place were given a prize and a dinner in grateful recognition.

"The *carradori*, or carters, were continually transporting stone from the quarries to the building yard of Palazzo Strozzi; in the period from November 28, 1495 to March 24, 1497, nearly 1,200 cart

Left View of Florence showing Santa Maria del Fiore, Palazzo Vecchio, the Uffizi, and the towers of the Bargello and the Badia.

Central Florence, seen from the hill of Bellosguardo.

loads of stone from the quarries of Boboli and Marignolle were supplied to the builders working on Palazzo Strozzi.

"The facade of Palazzo Rucellai, by Leon Battista Alberti, was entirely covered with *pietra forte* and featured a radically new idea: the facade was punctuated with pilaster strips. The decorative bands of diamond-shaped rings and bellying sails are finely carved.

"Alongside the fortified palazzo, or *palazzo munito*, a second type arose, the *palazzo fiorito*, a term that translates roughly to flowering palazzo. This type of palazzo was predominantly characterized by plastered masonry. Let us mention just one distinctive example: Palazzo Quaratesi. The lower section is composed of rough ashlars, while the upper part is covered with plaster, broken up here and there by enchanting bits of decoration around the windows. This decoration, sadly, is in very poor shape."

Again Rodolico recalls—in discussing the use of stone for construction in Florentine monumental architecture—that: "In effect, from the sixteenth century onward, all of the various types of stone that we have discussed here were used to some extent. Two masterpieces of the Cinquecento were built wholly of *pietra forte*: the courtyard of Palazzo Pitti and the bridge called Ponte a Santa Trinita; both were built with stone from the quarry in the Boboli gardens. The quarry in question was at one point

reopened for a number of years in order to excavate stone needed to repair the bridge. The facades of many baroque churches were built with *pietra forte*, ranging from the church of San Gaetano to the church of Santa Trinita, though the church of Ognissanti had a facade of *pietra serena*, which was replaced with travertine in the nineteenth century.

"Often different types of stone were used in the same construction. In the Loggia del Mercato Nuovo, the columns of *pietra serena* were firmly set around with pillars of *pietra forte*. In Palazzo Bartolini Salimbeni (1529), the facade facing Piazza Santa Trinita is made of *pietra forte*, while the facade overlooking Via Porta Rossa is built of *pietra bigia* ["grey" stone] save for the decorative motifs on the elegant portal, which bears the motto *Per non dormire* (Lest we sleep) carved in *pietra forte*. And the three types of stone are even more mixed in the eighteenth-century facade of the Arcispedale di Santa Maria Nuova. A distinct preference for *pietra serena* can be sensed in the nineteenth century— from the neoclassical architecture of Pasquale Poccianti to the classical-style work of Giuseppe Poggi; the preference became stronger where the tradition of Brunelleschi was particularly strong.

"Thus, the many different types of stone quarried on

The hill of San Miniato al Monte. In the foreground, note the towers of the Bargello and the Badia, and the church of San Filippo Neri.

either side of the Arno in Florence, stones which over the centuries flowed in great volume into the greater and lesser buildings erected, are now the source of a discordant uniformity, a creation of exquisite beauty."

The age of maturity: modifications and further improvements

In his study *I palazzi di Firenze nella storia e nell'arte,* Ginori Lisci devoted systematic attention to the construction of the palazzi, offering explanations and comparisons that take into account the growing prosperity of Florence and the specific dynamics of the Florentine economy. The same author singled out the seven most famous palazzi—Palazzo Medici, Palazzo Rucellai, Palazzo Pitti, Palazzo Pazzi, Palazzo Antinori, Palazzo Strozzi, and Palazzo Gondi. These palazzi, or at least their most important sections, were built between 1440 and 1500, that is, in the second half of the Quattrocento. The architecture of that period was renewed by Brunelleschi, Alberti, Michelozzo, and later by Giuliano da Sangallo and Simone del Pollaiolo, known as the Cronaca. It seems appropriate to note that, with this new, refined architectural typology the interior/exterior exchange, already present in the transitional palazzi with the large loggias crowning the roof, found a larger and more organic solution in the systematic introduction of a

courtyard. The courtyard, counterpart of the cloister in the religious architecture of convents, almost hearkens back to the ideology of the Roman home (consider the *impluvium,* where a cistern was used to gather rainwater from the roofs). Now, however, the courtyard had become the single distinctive feature that, by size and nature, indicated a larger structure, as is the case with the Florentine palazzo.

Later, in the first half of the Cinquecento, there was a further renovation of architecture, led by the Cronaca and Baccio d'Agnolo. The courtyard and the loggia became the fundamental compositional elements, and exterior decorations began to appear in the form of either *graffiti* or paintings. Inside, the staircases became less steep. The risers diminished from 8.5–10 inches to the more usual 6.5–7 inches, and in some cases were as low as 5.5 inches; as a result, climbing or descending the stairs became a more dignified act, almost a processional ritual. *Grottesche,* (grotesques) were introduced. These decorations, revived at the turn of the sixteenth century, dated back to Nero's Domus Aurea, or great villa, which was unearthed in that period. They include mythical figures, animals, plants, fables, and interpretive stylistic elements of polymorphic fantasies (see the delightful essay by André Chastel, "La Grotesque," *Le Promeneur,* Paris 1988). Andrea di Cosimo Feltrini was a major figure in the development of grotesque

decorations in Florence. The parabola of the Florentine palazzi came to an end in the second half of the Cinquecento, with the work of Ammannati and Buontalenti, and with the spread of *inginocchiate* windows, balconies, and portrait busts on the facade; these were elements of mediation with contemporary Roman architecture, which was about to dominate Florentine architecture, with the assistance of Gherardo Silvani. The matter of *inginocchiate* windows has been treated a number of times. These are large, usually ground-floor, "kneeling" windows, so-called because of the scrolled corbels that support the windows' heavy sills (see Palazzo Medici Riccardi, page 51). Similarly, the question of the palazzo facade's customary asymmetry has been much considered. This was often the result of the incorporation and rebuilding of medieval buildings, which tended to have lots 10 or 12 *braccia* wide, facing the street (1 *braccio* was 58.4 cm. or about 23 inches); this topic has been throughly studied by G. Luigi Maffei and Giancarlo Cataldi, who were both students of Gianfranco Caniggia. Here is what Giuseppe Marchini had to say (from "Le Finestre Inginocchiate," *Antichità Viva,* I, 1976): "as an aside in his life of Giovanni da Udine, Vasari speaks of a work by Giovanni; after mentioning the loggia that stood at the corner of the palazzo that was built in Florence at the behest of Cosimo de' Medici the Elder, Vasari

described how this loggia had been 'closed with a design by Michelangelo Buonarroti, who made a little room out of it, with two *inginocchiate* windows, the first ones built in that manner with iron-work on the outside of the palazzo. Vasari returned to this topic in his life of Michelangelo,

stating specifically that he had made a model of the *inginocchiate* windows for the rooms that stand at the corner of Palazzo Medici, with the room that Giovanni da Udine stuccoed and painted, a widely praised piece of work."

The second passage is dropped in, almost a parenthetical aside as Vasari

View from the Arno toward the
Porta a San Niccolò and San
Miniato.

recounts the ordeal Michelangelo went through when quarrying marble to be used in the facade of San Lorenzo. Based on this information and other, even more decisive facts, we can place the date of this episode at about 1517. Vasari must have known quite a bit about it, for that matter, since he worked less than twenty years later on completing the pictorial decorations of that same room, created by walling in the loggia.

This information has been universally accepted as accurate; likewise, the term *finestre inginocchiate* can safely be considered to have been coined by Giorgio Vasari, even though the somewhat pedantic Giuseppe Del Rosso has tried to attribute it to Cosimo Bartoli; in fact, however, Bartoli's *Ragionamenti Accademici* was printed sixteen years after the first edition of Vasari's *Vite* (Lives of the Most Eminent Italian Painters, Sculptors and Architects). In fact, even the second edition of the *Vocabolario della Crusca*, an early and authoritative Italian dictionary, names Vasari for the first citation of the term.

Giuseppe Marchini produced an exceedingly useful work on the history and development of the medieval division of property ("Facciate Fiorentine," *Antichità Viva*, III, 1978): In fact, the medieval division of property, conducted on a massive scale during the period of urban expansion that saw Florence spread out beyond the second-to-last ring of walls at the turn of the thirteenth century,

was based on a standard of ten *braccia* of street-front facade, equivalent to 5.8 meters [about 19 feet], with only a few variants, slightly wider or narrower.

"In any case, these lots—which constituted the minimum unitary grid size for a single home—tended to encourage an interior division of space into two rooms on the ground floor, which thus required two vertical bays of windows on the elevation: French windows on the ground floor, and two windows on the upper floor or floors. Entire streets in Florence still present a unbroken series of facades punctuated in precisely this fashion, especially in the poorer sections of town where the original layout of the buildings has survived relatively intact despite the passage of time and inevitable renovations [...]. Now, if we observe cases like that of Palazzo Rucellai, cases in which several lots were combined to erect a single building, we find that the binary rhythm or structure of the previously existing houses has generally been maintained with an even number of openings or vertical bays; the front door or portal usually remains in an asymmetrical position. The cost of rebuilding was one of the strongest arguments for respecting the original layout of apertures and solid wall; in the final analysis the layout of windows generally corresponded to the arrangement of the rooms, something that is rarely governed by an over-

all ideal symmetry (the only exception is found in cases of large buildings erected *a fundamentis*). And so we find palazzi and palazzetti with an array of vertical bays of windows that ranged in number from four to six to eight, or even more. Among them we can surely count famous or distinctive examples, such as Palazzo Bardi-Serzelli, Palazzo Antinori, and Palazzo Horne; another instance is the solemn line of palazzi on Via Maggio. Entire streets are dominated by this *a due* ["two-by-two" sequencing]; one example is the aristocratic Via Larga, now called Via Cavour, in which there are virtually no exceptions. When grandeur exceeded certain limits, in some cases the builders would rely on the binary rhythm, or even strain to attain it with symmetrical double doors, based on the example of Palazzo Rucellai, which otherwise would have been roundly ignored in the Florentine milieu, as if it spoke an unacceptable language."

The progress and reorganization of the Florentine palazzo came about in accordance with the ideas of the Cronaca and Baccio d'Agnolo. What followed was the period of the Tuscan grand duchy, with Giorgio Vasari as unrivalled mastermind, enjoying the full favor of Cosimo de' Medici. Among the names cited—in conjunction with Cosimo, Francesco, and Ferdinando de' Medici—are Vasari, Ammannati, and Buontalenti: the cream of the crop of sixteenth-century

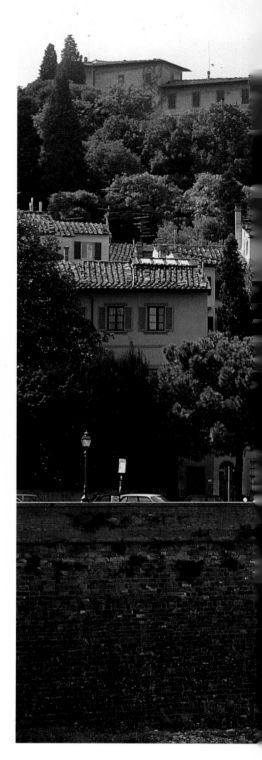

A view of the Torrigiani embankment on the Arno, dominated by the hill of San Giorgio, one of the first areas to be enclosed within the walled perimeter in Oltrarno.

Following pages
A view of the Arno embankment
with the distinctive structure of
Palazzo Corsini, the Ponte a Santa
Trinita, Palazzo Feroni, and the
Torre di Arnolfo in the
background.

Florentine architecture. Plastered walls were replaced by rusticated stone; facades began to be symmetrical (the result of a less restrictive rebuilding); windows were no longer topped with archivolts, but rather, canonically, with triangular or curved pediments; large *inginocchiate* windows became the protagonists of the ground floor order; and the terrace or balcony was introduced (a feature that was entirely new to Florentine culture). In the atrium of the Florentine palazzo, after the entry portal and above the iron gratework—in much the same way as a lunette—we begin to see *cartelloni* or *bandelloni*, upon which was affixed the family coat-of-arms, painted in oil on a wooden panel. Lastly, the large stone heraldic crest was placed at the corner of the palazzo.

Urban gardens

Florentine gardens can now boast quite a substantial architectural historiography all their own, and yet they have been studied chiefly, if not exclusively, in relation to villas; only secondarily have gardens been examined as part of the urban palazzo. Bocchi-Cinelli and Ginori Lisci make some mention of the city garden, but it was not until 1981 that the first systematic guide to urban gardens was published. The book, *Guida ai Giardini Urbani di Firenze*, was edited by Vincenzo Cazzato and Massimo De Vico Fallani, and lists nearly all of these singular creations.

Let us mention, as an example, the former garden of Palazzo di San Clemente, which belonged to Luigi of Toledo, brother of the grand duchess Eleonora; Vasari thought the garden was designed by Francesco Camilliani. Here is a presentation of it (Cazzato):

"Composed to an urban scale, it adopted a cross-shape that referred to archetypal urban layouts; in this way, the garden became the achievement of 'a despotic dream of order and total control of space, which was unattainable in the historical plan of the city.' (P. Rinaldi).

"A different sort of furnishing was found on the two drives: the axis perpendicular to the palazzo, with high espaliers of shrubbery, concluding in two enormous arrays of nicely pruned

holm-oaks; the other, transverse axis was lined by trees with tall trunks and a double row of columns, and ended at the monumental fountain by Camilliani. This fountain-island—elliptical in shape and built on three levels, adorned with statues of river gods and agrarian deities—

was sold in 1573 to the city of Palermo and erected in the center of the Piazza Pretoria. The smaller fountain, at the intersection of the two drives, served on the other hand as a 'perspectival backdrop or vanishing point for the longitudinal axis, as well as a visual hinge for the transverse axis. The double perspectival series of the side avenue, revolving around the fountain as if on the fulcrum of a movable backdrop', could thus 'break in with its sequence of vignettes—in a sort of visible scene

change—on the field of perception of a visitor, which until that point had been hemmed in by the great boxwood hedges, and focused on the optical attractor of the central fountain'. (P. Rinaldi). In 1636, the garden became the property of Ortensia Guadagni, widow

of a Salviati. Her brother, Tommaso Guadagni, purchased other houses on Via S. Sebastiano, and hired Gherardo Silvani to design a new *Casino* [country lodge].

"In 1777, the palazzo was sold, with its garden, to Prince Charles Edward Stuart, the Young Pretender; when the prince died, the estate was purchased by Simone Velluti Zati, duke of S. Clemente (1788).

"Over the course of the nineteenth century, the size of the garden was considerably reduced, due to the construction of several roads.

"The palazzo now belongs to the University of Florence."

More recently, Maria Chiara Pozzana has assembled—in a charming little album illustrated with watercolors by Mauro Falzoni—an anthology of the city gardens of Florence. The album

well as considerable patience. This is because they are ruled by the seasons; also the very perception of those gardens is rendered difficult, not only by the fact that they are hidden away in Florence, but also by the fact that the pace of life has become so hectic, in a city

there are certain times that are better than others. A garden is a work of art that cannot be enjoyed at all times. You must wait for the right season to enjoy the flowering of the azaleas in the garden of Palazzo Della Gherardesca, to glimpse the blooming begonias in the

not for those in a hurry."

And so we return to the palazzo and the culture of the men and women who built it. They had a unique enthusiasm for creating in order to justify their existence. This quality is not the same as the opulent ostentation of great potentates or monarchs. One understands in this way, and only in this way, the enthusiasm of scholars such as Janet Ross or Richard Goldthwaite, who, more than half a century apart, devoted so much of their time and understanding to the study of the palazzi and the architecture of the Florentine Renaissance. Goldthwaite clearly laid out in a preface the various components that made the construction of a palazzo possible: ". . . the various forces of production that went into building are surveyed: organization of work, the building-material industries, the labor force, and the aesthetic component, the architect. Because construction by its very nature requires many different kinds of workers, ranging from unskilled manual laborers to highly talented artists, some working as day laborers and others as small entrepreneurs, this description of the industry offers, in effect, a cross section of working-class society in Renaissance Florence."

includes, to mention only a few, the gardens of palazzi Capponi [Via Gino Capponi], Budini Gattai, Pandolfini, Medici Riccardi, Valfonda, Corsini sul Prato, Orti Oricellari, Serristori, and Frescobaldi. As Pozzana wrote: "In Florence it seems rather that the city gardens were deliberately concealed behind the facades of the buildings, or in some cases, behind high walls or gates that hide them from view. It takes a great deal of effort to see them, or perhaps we should say unearth them, as

that is polluted by noise as well as by fumes. To observe a garden requires the right frame of mind; to understand a garden also requires a certain degree of concentration. None of this corresponds to the hasty and distracted approach that is common to those who live in the center of Florence.

"The problem is not only that most gardens are private, and therefore difficult to tour (and this remains a problem to be solved). It is also that a garden is not always 'willing' to be seen,

gardens of Borgo Pinti through the occasional open portal, to see the wisteria clinging in violet clusters to the walls of houses, or to recognize the arrival of autumn from the scent of the osmanthus. Gardens are part of nature, and nature cannot be hurried along; thus, you cannot necessarily tour or even look at a garden whenever you choose.

"For all the progress in plant husbandry, every garden has its own natural schedules; gardens are not for everyone, and certainly

Such a civic, social, and economic mixture was never again to find such favorable conditions in all of Europe.

The Public Palazzo
An example of history and architecture

Michelozzo, Palazzo Medici Riccardi,
inner courtyard.

In the cities of the Middle Ages, the palazzo was not featured in the architecture of private homes. That is to say, there were no palazzi that belonged to individual families, however rich or influential a family might be. Powerful families tended to live in groups of houses that were adjacent to each other, interconnected, and grouped around a shared interior courtyard; these houses came to constitute independent city blocks. Features were added to make them safe from attack: towers were added, windows were made small and narrow, the houses rose high and sheer into the sky.

Palazzi, rather, were buildings erected to contain the magistracies and all the officials of government, in towns and cities that were very proud of their communal institutions and their ancient freedoms, which they identified with their palazzi. The palazzo, therefore, was a public building, the hub of political life.

Florence was no exception to this rule. The first palazzo built in Florence was the Palazzo del Capitano del Popolo (1255), later known as the Bargello in recognition of the sole offical representative

The Sala dei Gigli (Hall of Lilies) in Palazzo Vecchio is named for the distinctive gilt fleurs-de-lys on a blue background that decorate the walls in commemoration of an alliance between Florence and the royal house of France. Worthy of particular note are the coffered ceiling, the portal by Benedetto da Maiano, and the frescoes by Domenico Ghirlandaio (1481–85). The frescoes depict *Saint Zanobi in Majesty, with Saint Lawrence and Saint Stephen.* Flanking them are six illustrious men from classical times: Brutus, Mutius Scaevola, Camillus, Decius, Scipio, and Cicero.

The renowned facade of Palazzo Vecchio, with its notable rustication, elegant twin-light mullioned windows, crenelated crown, and great tower, known as the Torre di Arnolfo. The two types of parapets, Guelph and Ghibelline (swallowtail and flat crown), symbolize in this public palace the unification of the entire citizenry. On either side of the main entrance, note the copy of Michelangelo's *David,* and the group of *Hercules and Cacus,* by Baccio Bandinelli. For many years, though, the main entrance was considered to be the one on the north side of the building, on the left in this view.

Above The Sala di Cosimo I, on the second floor, features frescoes that depict Cosimo in the midst of illustrious personages of his time. In the medallions are portraits of Eleonora of Toledo, and the grand duke's children.

Left The Sala di Clemente I is entirely decorated with episodes from the life and teachings of the pope. Of particular note is a fresco of the siege of Florence in 1530.

The chapel of the Apartment of Eleonora on the second floor is entirely painted by Bronzino (ca. 1564). Depicted are *Stories of Moses*, including this detail on the ceiling. This was one of Bronzino's most demanding projects.

of the Commune, or city government, who had previously been obliged to make do with improvised lodgings and offices. The most prestigious palazzo was built just over thirty years later, on behalf of the Priori delle Arti, the heads of the various guilds; this Palazzo dei Priori was later named the Palazzo della Signoria.

The Priori were representatives of powerful guilds. These guilds encompassed a good portion of the city's population, organized according to trade or craft. In time, they became arbiters of city life, and with the passing decades, they became, in practice, the single most influential magistracy in Florence. And so, when the decision was made to build an appropriate building to house them, the city turned to the most highly esteemed architect in Florence, a master builder of public works at the end of the thirteenth century, Arnolfo di Cambio. This pupil of Nicola Pisano was now past fifty, and had already completed outstanding and lovely buildings; at this time, he was engaged in the construction of the new cathedral, Santa Maria del Fiore.

Arnolfo planned a precise network of links and relationships in the context of a more general urban renewal. The cathedral and the Palazzo dei Priori would be symmetrically located at opposite ends of an axis (along a radius connected to the ancient ring of the walled perimeter) constituted by Via dei Calzaiuoli. These two buildings would thus establish a monumental com-

plex occupying the heart of the city, in which the two great authorities—church and state—were symbolically united. Each would be symbolized in a deftly managed interplay of volume and bulk: the two preeminent structures were the dome, on one side, and the tower, on the other.

But when Arnolfo began work on the Palazzo dei Priori, in 1298, he suddenly found himself fettered by limitations of space and foregone decisions, imposed by existing circumstances. The Florentine historian Giovanni Villani offers a clear account of it in his book, *Cronica Universale* (Book VIII, chapter XXVI).

First of all, he had to keep in mind that in the area selected for the construction of the new building had once stood the houses of the Uberti family. This family had been a leading force in the Ghibelline

The Salone dei Cinquecento (the Great Hall of the Five Hundred) is one of the most monumental halls in any Italian *palazzo pubblico*. It was built in 1495 by the Cronaca to serve as a meeting place for the two thousand members of the Consiglio Grande del Popolo (Great Council of the Populace). This council had just been established on the crest of the new and fervid populist ideas of Savonarola. At the behest of Cosimo I, this hall was then adapted for receptions and public audiences. Between 1560 and 1572 it was entirely decorated by Vasari and his assistants with paintings depicting the great deeds of the grand duke Cosimo I. In the center of the ceiling, which is split into thirty-nine panels, the eye is immediately drawn to *The Apotheosis of Cosimo* (left). Unquestionably, one of the best known paintings in the room is *The Assault on Pisa* (below). Between 1865 and 1871 when Florence was, briefly, Italy's capital, the Salone dei Cinquecento was used as the meeting hall of the Chamber of Deputies of the Kingdom of Italy.

faction, outlawed when the opposing Guelphs finally and definitively triumphed. As was customary in such cases, all property of the Uberti family had been declared forfeit and confiscated; their buildings had been razed to the ground. Where those buildings had once stood, it was decreed that a plaza be built, and there was a total and inviolable prohibition against building on the plaza, lest the houses of the Uberti family be rebuilt. And that was not all. Not far away stood the church of San Piero Scheraggio, which, as a house of worship, could not be demolished.

Between these two locations stood the houses of the Foraboschi family, with the towering Torre della Vacca, which the city government hurriedly purchased. They were torn down, and in their place the new Palazzo dei Priori soon rose.

Constrained by these precise strictures, Arnolfo took the Torre della Vacca as a starting point; upon the foundations of this tower, he built the new Torre dei Priori, now known as the Torre di Arnolfo. At the base of this tower, Arnolfo built the majestic parallelepiped structure that constituted the original core of the building, surrounding a porticoed courtyard which was later renovated in the fifteenth century by Michelozzo. The true facade of the building was originally the short side, facing north, with the portal placed appropriately at dead-center. It was not until many

Also on the second floor is the Quartiere di Leone X, the quarters of Pope Leo X. It comprises the Sala di Leone X, which is decorated with episodes from the life of Giovanni de' Medici, a cardinal who then became pope.

The Studiolo di Francesco I, a small study, is truly a little architectural jewel; it was built by Giorgio Vasari between 1570 and 1572 as a den for the scholarly, art-loving ruler. The panels on the ceiling are by Francesco Morandini; the portraits of Cosimo and Eleonora in the lunettes are by Bronzino; the doors of the cupboards were painted by various Mannerist artists in the sixteenth century. Among the bronze statues situated in niches is *Apollo* by Giambologna, and *Venus* by Ammannati.

decades later that the main entrance became the present one, on the side facing west, opening more directly onto the square as it finally took form, closed off by the Loggia dei Lanzi. Because it had not originally been designed as the main portal, it was asymmetrically located with respect to the new facade, as was the tower; and so it has remained to the present day.

In the construction of what was to become Florence's public palace *par excellence*, Arnolfo remained faithful to the typical features of medieval civil architecture: the tower, the courtyard with portico, and the vaulted hall on the ground floor, divided into two aisles. Directly corresponding to this hall, on the floor above, was the Sala del Consiglio. Originally one entered this hall by an exterior staircase, as was common.

Alongside these features of medieval civil architecture, however, Arnolfo added other elements that were taken directly from military architecture: the galleries of the eaves, merlons or parapets, and the tower itself, conceived as a defensive structure, completely solid, unbroken by windows; it was built to hold the bell, which rang to announce sessions of the Consiglio, or Council. The bell in question had previously hung in the church of San Piero Scheraggio, mentioned previously.

Arnolfo thus created a homogeneous structure with a precise and well-defined identity, despite the variety of its

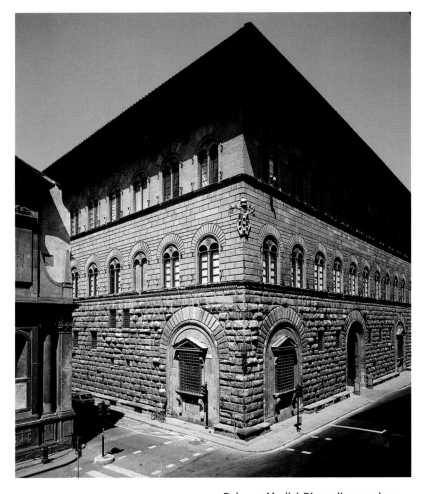

Palazzo Medici Riccardi served as an archetype for all Florentine palazzi that were used as private residences throughout the fifteenth century. It has a brilliant and severe facade, comprising three orders of ashlars—rustic, flat, and seamless. The windows are centered and may well be copies of the windows in Palazzo Vecchio, and the building has two sharply defined cornicework stringcourses. In 1512 the loggia at the ground-floor corner was sealed up; replacing it are two *fenestre inginocchiate* ("kneeling" windows, because of the scrolls beneath the sill) designed by Michelangelo.

component parts. This building rose majestically above the surrounding city; the tower stood about 317 feet tall, while the building itself stood about 141 feet at the uppermost gallery. Construction was definitively completed around 1330. Since then, the Palazzo dei Priori, or Palazzo del Popolo, later known as the Palazzo della Signoria—and, with the passing of the centuries, as Palazzo Vecchio, or the old palace—came to constitute a veritable prototype for the town halls of many Tuscan cities (Scarperia, Montepulciano, Volterra, and others). The halls of this building uninterruptedly housed the chief authorities and officials of Florentine government (the halls were decorated, frescoed, and renovated in many different phases, by artists of genius, foremost among them Giorgio Vasari). The building survived revolutions and transitions of all sorts, from the Seigneury to the Grand Duchy, to the Kingdom, and finally to the modern-day Republic.

Even now, seven centuries after its construction, Palazzo Vecchio houses the offices of the mayor of Florence and the city council.

Among the numerous institutional changes that affected the Palazzo della Signoria, one of the most significant was certainly the advent of the powerful Medici family at the helm of the state. This event was anything but traumatic or sudden; it was the result of a patient brick-by-brick process,

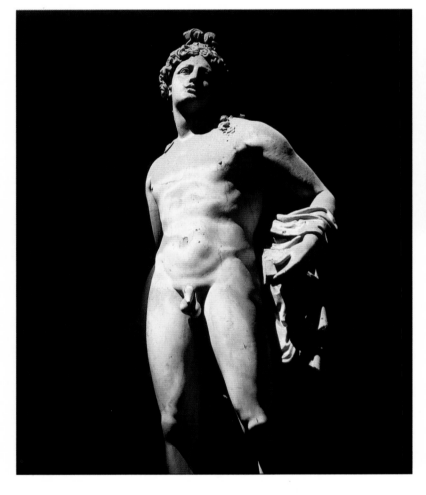

The courtyard of Palazzo Medici Riccardi is a rhythmic, three-part masterpiece consisting of the ground-floor portico, the second-floor facade, and the Ionic colonnade of the third-floor loggia. The *graffiti* are by Maso di Bartolomeo; the medallions on the architrave above the arches are attributed to Bertoldo di Giovanni. Over the centuries the courtyard has accumulated numerous artworks, sarcophagi, statues, plaques, and busts; some were taken from the exterior walls of the Baptistery, and others from the various homes and estates of the Riccardi family; others still came from the acquisitions made in Rome by the marchese Francesco Riccardi at the turn of the eighteenth century. On the side opposite the entrance stands *Orpheus*, a remarkable sixteenth-century statue by Baccio Bandinelli.

characteristically concrete, as was to be expected from a family of merchants. It was the work of many different members of the Medici family.

Certainly, a decisive contribution came from Cosimo, known as Cosimo the Elder, who was the son of Giovanni di Bicci, who can rightly be considered the founder of this family's fortunes. He had quickly understood that, in order to obtain a position of real power and preeminence in Florence, it was necessary to act with extreme discretion. There could be no ostentation of luxury and power. He would have to manuever behind the scenes, manipulating the city's public life while making a show of respect and devotion to the most important Republican institutions.

Cosimo transformed this intuition into a full-bodied political program; he never abandoned it, and he successfully handed it on to his own descendants. In fact, no Medici, until the fourth decade of the sixteenth century, ever held any public office—not even Lorenzo the Magnificent—even though the Medici family had held absolute power over Florence for nearly a century. Cosimo clung to this rule even when, around 1440, he decided that the time had come to build a palazzo worthy of his family's enormous ambitions. By this time other noble families had inaugurated the tradition of a large residence as a demonstration of financial might, and as a safe and fortified haven for the immediate family.

Left A large panel bearing the key of the Riccardi heraldic crest.

Below and opposite A view of the courtyard, which is certainly one of Michelozzo's greatest masterpieces; on the facing page, the view looking through to the portal that opens onto Via Cavour.

The marble base of the statue of *Orpheus* shows the heraldic attributes of the Medici.

Thus, Palazzo Medici was meant to meet specific requirements: it would have to appear stern, sober, and elegant from the exterior, both massive and impressive. Yet it must not betray the luxury and elegance which could be expressed, on the inside, with greater freedom; the life of the family, when protected from prying eyes, could be made quite comfortable.

At first, at least in part from considerations of prestige, but also because of the architect's unquestioned talent, Cosimo turned to Filippo Brunelleschi, the architect who had, over the course of a few decades, altered the face of the city of Florence, turning it into a true Renaissance city. Brunelleschi produced a design and a wooden model of singular beauty: a building with a square floor plan, with nine windows on each face. According to Brunelleschi's plans, it would stand directly across from the church of San Lorenzo.

This was an ambitious project, and the outlay would have been enormous. Above all, it clashed with the discreet public image that Cosimo had chosen to adopt. Cosimo rejected the plan, more with a view to stifling envy than out of concern for the expense, as Vasari put it in his *Lives of the Most Eminent Italian Painters, Sculptors and Architects*. Instead, he turned to another architect who had also shown uncommon talent; in time, this architect was to prove to be the most skillful interpreter of the wishes and ambitions of

Preceding pages In Palazzo Medici Riccardi, the second floor was split into independent apartments from the beginning. Cosimo the Elder and Lorenzo the Magnificent both lived in this palazzo. It was a gathering place for intellectuals, artists, and scientists. The first room is now part of the apartment of the President of the Italian Republic, and the second is part of the apartment of the Prefect.

Opposite Perhaps the most distinctive decorative elements in this palazzo are the splendid tapestries created specially for the Medici family; several of the tapestries hang in the dining room.

A small vestibule with elegant curtains leads into a bedroom.

Detail of a tapestry showing Moses shattering the Ten Commandments.

Cosimo. It was Michelozzo.

Michelozzo, after initial contacts with Lorenzo Ghiberti and Donatello, had demonstrated a growing interest in Brunelleschi's approach. If Brunelleschi's work was sometimes rather abstract, Michelozzo moved it in the direction of the massive and powerful walls, stone, and

facades in which the lines and surfaces were clearly marked and well defined.

Michelozzo had already worked for Cosimo once, when he renovated the convent of San Marco. On that occasion he had shown himself to be equal to the most demanding tasks.

And so, beginning in 1444, construction was undertaken of the Palazzo Medici of Via Larga (now Via Cavour). The architecture still maintains the typically medieval concept of the corner view as the fundamental perspective, with an innovative approach and original development of the volumes.

The palazzo, in its original version had a main facade that overlooked Via Larga, with ten vertical bays of windows and three portals. (In the second half of the seventeenth century, the Riccardi family, which had purchased the building from the Medici in 1659—hence the modern name of Palazzo Medici Riccardi—enlarged it considerably, which resulted in the destruction of all the various annexes—stables, storehouses, kitchens—and the elimination of the carriage gateway.)

The sheer upward thrust appeared to be in sharp contrast with the massive jutting cornice, intentionally designed to heighten the impression of stern power created by the gradated rustication along the three stories. In order to reinforce further the idea of a fortress-palazzo, a safe haven rather than an elegant residence, it was decided not to provide the ground

A typical drawing room, used for receiving guests (left); a charming dining room (below); and a parlor with handsomely frescoed walls, with classical subjects and architectural elements (opposite).

Following pages Remarkable frescoes were painted by Luca Giordano around 1683 for the baroque gallery, built during the general enlargement of the building undertaken by the Riccardi family between 1670 and 1688. The frescoes depict the *Apotheosis of the Medici Dynasty*(page 62), and the *Apotheosis of Divine Wisdom* (page 63). The paintings that adorn the walls were painted by Antonio Domenico Gabbiani.

floor—traditionally devoted to facilities (kitchen and bathroom) rather than living quarters—with windows. Windows were only added in the sixteenth century; they were designed by none other than Michelangelo, and are markedly different from the centered twin-light mullioned windows that make such an elegant and lovely display on the second and third floors.

Without a doubt, one of Michelozzo's finest creations is the courtyard of the palazzo, conceived in a transitional step between the convent cloister and the medieval courtyard. It has a lovely, ground-floor columned atrium, and an exquisite third-floor gallery with an Ionic colonnade. Of particular note is the painstaking decoration of the architrave that runs around the entire courtyard. This courtyard was soon taken as a model for many palazzo courtyards built after the middle of the fifteenth century.

Also worthy of note is the small enclosed garden, meant to be used by the family alone, and still quite in keeping with the medieval atmosphere. The arrangement of the interior, on the other hand, is much more modern; the rooms are connected one to another along straight axes, so that each wing constitutes a self-contained apartment comprising living room, bedchamber, antechamber, and study. Cosimo was especially fond of the apartment overlooking the garden, while Lorenzo the Magnificent chose to live in the apartment

A hallway (left) features an original fireplace with the Medici crest (above).
Opposite The garden was originally conceived by Michelozzo as an enclosed space reached by an open passageway at the center of the wall that encloses the portico, in accordance with a purely medieval style.

overlooking Via Larga because it was directly connected to the principal receiving hall and the splendid chapel that had been designed by Michelozzo and decorated by Benozzo Gozzoli.

Palazzo Medici remained the urban residence of Florence's "reigning" family until 1540, which is to say, as long as it appeared advisable to adhere to Cosimo's avowed policy of separating the Medici's image as a private family from any public office. In 1537, however, another Cosimo, a grand-nephew, was officially declared duke and ruler of Florence. From that moment onward all caution appeared superfluous, and it became advisable, indeed, that the Medici family should move into the palazzo that had become symbolic of power in Florence, the Palazzo della Signoria, as Palazzo Vecchio was called in that period. Palazzo Medici was destined to be the home of the cadets and widows of the dynasty; in time it was sold to the Riccardi family, as explained above. All the same, because of the elegance of Palazzo Medici, because of its prestige—reflected in the name of its owners—and because of its long-standing role in the context of Florentine social life, it never lost its status as the model for most private homes in the fifteenth and sixteenth centuries. Many who had built homes in that period openly admitted that they wished their homes to rival Palazzo Medici in dignity. Today, the Florence Prefecture occupies

The impressive facade of Palazzo Pitti, with its rustication and identically recurring windows and portals makes it impossible to distinguish the early central structure of the home of Luca Pitti, designed by Brunelleschi, and the later enlargement, done by Ammannati in the sixteenth century. The two so-called side wings were added in the second half of the eighteenth century, based on plans by the architect Giuseppe Ruggieri. *Above, left* Also attributed to Ammannati, and certainly dating from the sixteenth century, are the windows on the ground floor with lion's heads wearing the grand-ducal crown. Note the singular addition of a marble basin.

Between 1558 and 1570, Ammannati built the splendid courtyard, enclosed on three sides by the palazzo, and fully open on the fourth side, overlooking the garden. For centuries, this courtyard was the site of the famous spectacles and performances (naumachias, tourneys, plays, and dramas) staged by the court of the Medici.

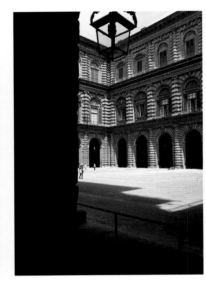

the building; in the section added later by the Riccardi is the Biblioteca Riccardiana, a highly respected library.

When Grand Duke Cosimo moved into Palazzo della Signoria, he was newly married to Eleonora of Toledo, the young daughter of the Viceroy of Naples. For the duke and duchess it was quite a simple matter to settle into those sections of the palazzo that are still known as the *Appartamenti di Cosimo* and the *Appartamenti di Eleonora.* Before long, the marriage proved to be an extraordinarily prolific one: Eleonora gave birth, one after the other, to Maria, Francesco, Isabella, Giovanni, Lucrezia, Anna, Pedricco, Garzia, Ferdinando, and Pietro. Palazzo della Signoria, which had most certainly not been designed to accommodate a family, much less a large and growing family, soon proved inadequate. Cosimo began to look around for a new home. The home he sought was to have two qualities—it should be large enough to accommodate his numerous offspring, and it should not be too far away from the heart of political power in Florence, which in any case remained the Palazzo della Signoria.

His choice was the large house built by Luca Pitti, on the Colle di Boboli, in Oltrarno. Eleonora purchased it in 1549 for the price of 10,000 florins. Oddly enough, this great palazzo maintained the name of its first owner over the centuries, even though he had inhabited

The rear facade of Palazzo Pitti was left unfinished and rough in the fifteenth century, in direct contact with the hill behind it. The architect Ammannati gave it its present-day appearance, and added the balcony. The obelisk that stands in the foreground once stood in the center of the Amphitheater in the park. The granite basin comes from the Baths of Caracalla in Rome.

There are two main fountains in the Boboli Gardens—the magnificent, highly architectural garden designed by Tribolo, Ammannati, Buontalenti, and Alfonso Parigi. The first is the so-called Vivaio del Nettuno, a large basin featuring a statue of the sea-god Neptune by Stoldo Lorenzi (1565). The second fountain occupies the enormous Piazzale dell'Isolotto. This is the Fontana dell'Oceano, by Giambologna, a fountain with a personification of the Ocean in the center (this is a copy; the original is in the Bargello) surrounded by similar statues of the world's most important rivers.

Above A view of the lush vegetation toward the hill of Bellosguardo.
Right The Anfiteatro, or Amphitheater. This seventeenth-century construction was the work of Alfonso Parigi, but was renovated in the eighteenth century.

it only briefly, and despite the fact that for centuries it would be the residence of the grand-ducal family, and—after the unification of Italy—a royal palace. It is still known as Palazzo Pitti.

Luca Pitti was an exceedingly wealthy merchant and a rival of the Medici family.

There are many exquisite statues decorating even the furthest corners of the Boboli Gardens; they stand high atop rich and elaborate pedestals, which are often decorated with allegorical scenes (far left). One of the most renowned statues, the *Bacchino*, or little Bacchus, greets visitors at the entrance; a little fountain depicts Pietro Barbino, the court midget who was particularly dear to Cosimo I (left). The group of *Apollo and Ceres*, by Baccio Bandinelli was created for one of the artificial grottoes built by Buontalenti in 1583, as were Michelangelo's *Prisoners* and Giambologna's *Venus.*

Shortly before 1450, Pitti asked Filippo Brunelleschi to build a new mansion for him. This home was to be lovelier than any other in Florence; it was to have windows larger than the portal of Palazzo Medici on Via Larga.

The location of the new palazzo was quite unusual, distant from the center of Florence and from the streets where the leading families generally built their homes.

Right The visitor enters the garden through the Porta di Bacco, and proceeds along one of the broad and airy paths, lined with shrubbery, that crisscross the entire garden.

Below Work on the Palazzina della Meridiana was begun in 1776 by Gaspare Maria Paoletti, continued by Giuseppe Cacialli, and completed by Pasquale Poccianti at the turn of the nineteenth century. The Palazzina was a new residence that joined onto the garden side of Palazzo Pitti.

It was to overlook the surrounding countryside, not far from the Porta Romana.

Brunelleschi completed his plans for the new palazzo in 1446, just before his death. The palazzo was built to his design. Many homes were confiscated and demolished in order to make room for rustication. Facing the square were three portals and a series of windows that were identical to the portals (this last was quite a new concept). Moreover, the three central arches of the second floor were left open, creating the usual loggia, while there was a corresponding gallery

Sala IV in the Museo degli Argenti (Hall Four of the Museum of Silver) was simply an enormous empty hall on the ground floor until 1635. In that year, the grand duke Ferdinand II—who was planning his wedding to Vittoria Della Rovere, the last surviving heir to the dynasty of the dukes of Urbino—ordered Giovanni da San Giovanni to fresco it. The ceiling is emblazoned with a spectacular allegory of the ducal wedding.

the new *piazza,* or square, the first to lie before a private palazzo. Palazzo Pitti was built upon an exceptionally strong rock foundation, capable of supporting so large and weighty a building. Brunelleschi conceived the central wing as a simple, grand structure, three stories tall, with a progressively (floor-by-floor) smoother in the rear facade, overlooking the countryside. On the whole, there is a clear impression of a building meant to be viewed from the front—an impression emphasized by the presence of the *piazza*—so that the emphasis was more on the layout of the surfaces and less on the creation of volumes. In the rear, because of the slope of

Left The series of paintings in this hall is meant as an indirect glorification of the Medici family; they specifically exalt its most illustrious member, Lorenzo the Magnificent.

The frescoes in Sala IV depict the Muses being expelled from Mount Parnassus and taking refuge under the protection of Lorenzo de' Medici (note the detail of the swan holding a decorative medallion depicting Lorenzo); Lorenzo returns the Muses to their ancient power and restores their lost splendor. Following the death of Giovanni da San Giovanni in 1636, the project was completed by other renowned painters, including Francesco Furini, Cecco Bravo, and Ottavio Vannini.

the hill, the second story was level with the garden behind it.

This, then, was a proud and impressive home, and a highly original piece of architecture. Work was interrupted in 1465, however, when the Pitti family fell into financial ruin. As soon as Cosimo and Eleonora purchased it, work resumed: Bartolomeo Ammannati was hired to enlarge the exterior and interior of the palazzo. He had the necessary stone quarried from the courtyard itself, and from the garden. Construction continued until 1570, and the original design by Brunelleschi was respected.

In the meantime, Niccolò Pericoli, known as the Tribolo, was overseeing work on the gardens, which—with the later work done under Buontalenti and Alfonso Parigi—acquired the appearance that was to make the Boboli Gardens famous throughout the world. In the centuries that followed, the facade was further enlarged, first by Giulio Parigi (1620) and later by his son Alfonso Parigi (1640). The two side wings were added between 1764 and 1783, according to plans by Giuseppe Ruggieri.

As early as 1565, and in just six months' time, Cosimo de' Medici attained one of his most pressing requirements. Giorgio Vasari had designed and built a monumental corridor that ran across the Arno, directly connecting Cosimo's apartments in the Palazzo della Signoria with the grand-ducal home of Palazzo

Pitti. Thus, the center of political power and the private residence, though distant from one another, were united, symbolically underscoring the fact that Florence was ruled, irrevocably and permanently, by the Medici. Florence now had a third palazzo, and a garden that

was a place for official reception and entertaining—a garden that was to become a model for many later gardens.

Nowadays, the palazzo houses the Museo degli Argenti, the Galleria Palatina, and the Galleria di Arte Moderna.

Left Sala III of the Museo degli Argenti was entirely decorated by Angelo Michele Colonna and Agostino Mitelli, beginning in 1536. The prevailing subject is trompe-l'oeil architecture, which extends across walls and ceiling in a series of purely imaginary constructions. In the light-blue top of the ceiling, allegorical scenes glorify the Medici family.
Also in this hall is the Stipo di Alemagna, a cabinet given to Ferdinand II in 1628.

Left and opposite The Sala IV was the first true Sala degli Argenti (treasure chamber), from which the museum gets its name. The museum holds a vast collection of silver, precious stones, jewelry, ivory, porcelain, fabrics, and glass, largely from the rich Medici collections, but also from the treasure of the Palatine Electress and private donations. Note in particular the famous fresco by Vannini that depicts Michelangelo displaying a sculpted faun's head to Lorenzo the Magnificent (left).

Before the Medici: the age of tower-houses

Palazzo Davanzati: Nuptial Chamber, detail of the wall fresco.

Palazzo Feroni

Over the course of the thirteenth century, Florence was riven by a series of bloody factional struggles, prompted by the fierce rivalry between the Guelphs and Ghibellines, and further degenerating into in-fighting between the two Guelph factions of the Whites (Bianchi) and the Blacks (Neri). During this period it was of special importance, especially for the most prominent families, to build a secure home. As a result, tower-houses were built, along with the stout fortified palazzi that looked like the strongholds that they in fact were. One of the chosen areas for these palazzi was the bank of the river Arno. Here the buildings could occupy a dominant position that was therefore easily defended; at the same time, if located near a bridge-head, the occupants could enjoy total control of a strategic point of communications.

Near one of these bridges, the Ponte a Santa Trinita, along the Borgo Santi Apostoli, the wealthy Spini family had most of its homes and real estate (the family was a leading presence in Florence as early as the thirteenth century). Members of the Arte

Palazzo Feroni overlooks the Arno on a line with the Ponte a Santa Trinita. Its stern and decidedly medieval appearance is unmistakable; note the crenelated parapets and the sharp outline of the stone. Palazzo Feroni originally had two towers, one at the corner of Piazza Santa Trinita, the other on the Arno; indeed, the street running along the river cut around the base of that tower in a wide arc. The first tower was eliminated in the eighteenth century; the second was demolished in 1823 in order to ease carriage traffic on the Lungarno.

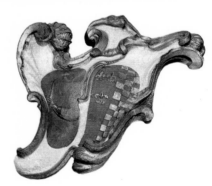

The heraldic crests that appear on the second floor refer to a marriage linking the Feroni family (left: the Feroni coat-of-arms) with the Bartolommei family.

del Cambio (Guild of the Moneychangers), the Spini family, through the family company, was for many years the banker for the pope, entitled to collect the tithes in Germany, Poland, Hungary, and Bohemia, and to make that income pay dividends. Many of them were also dis-

the Lungarno—to convert them into the stern and impressive palazzo-fortress we know today.

For the thirteenth century, this was quite a large building. From the planning stages—some say it was designed by Geri degli Spini; others believe the architect

tinguished in public office in Florence; one of the leading members of the family was Geri, who served at the end of the thirteenth century as lieutenant general under King Roberto of Naples, and ambassador to the Holy See under Pope Boniface VIII; he had also fought valiantly for Florence at the great battle of Campaldino. In fact, Messer Geri degli Spini, who was a successful merchant with a considerable fortune, decided to take advantage of the disastrous flood of 1299—which had damaged many of the houses he owned along

was Lapo Tedesco—the palazzo was split into two sections, to be used by the two branches of the family.

The wing that overlooked the Piazza Santa Trinita was inherited by the descendants of Geri degli Spini, who lived there until 1651, the year in which another Geri degli Spini, the son of Cristofano degli Spini, died without heirs. About this Geri degli Spini we know that when he inherited the building, the single facade covered three separate residences, the result of the combination of original thirteenth-century houses.

One of the most original rooms on the second floor is the bedroom, built at the turn of the eighteenth century by Lorenzo Merlini—a renowned sculptor, decorator, and architect of the period—at the behest of Simone da Bagnano. The vault of the main, square room was painted by Ranieri del Pace with scenes from a bacchanal (above). It is framed by stuccoes with putti modeled by Merlini himself. The alcove off the main room opens behind a basket arch and features a network of gilt stuccoes with stags (heraldic symbol of the owner's family) and festive putti, also according to plans by Merlini.

Between 1606 and 1611 this latter-day Geri degli Spini arranged to unify the various residential units. He then hired Barnardino Poccetti to decorate the rooms with series of frescoes. When this branch of the Spini family died out, their wing of the palazzo had a series of new owners: first Niccolò Guasconi, then Simone da Bagnano (whose family undertook a great many projects to improve the interior, moving the elegant little chapel to its present location). On the exterior, they gave the facade an odd Baroque appearance, with new pediments and decorations. Finally, in 1768 another wealthy merchant, the marchese Francesco Antonio Feroni purchased it.

In the meantime, the portion of the palazzo that overlooked the Arno—which had remained the property of the other branch of the Spini family—was transferred by marriage to the Del Tovaglia family by Camilla, the sole heir of Guglielmo di Jacopo degli Spini, in 1686. From that family the palazzo was passed to the Pitti family and then, in 1807, it was purchased by Francesco Feroni. By the nineteenth century, then, the palazzo had once again become the property of a single family, and it took their name. In 1834 the entire building became the property of another wealthy family, the Homberts. They converted it into an elegant and prestigious hotel. Its luxurious homes received illustrious guests such as Metternich and Czar

The renowned gallery, where the Spini family kept their collection of paintings—including work by Tintoretto, Andrea del Sarto, and Jacopo Palma the Elder—was renovated in the eighteenth century with paintings by Ranieri del Pace and stuccoes by Merlini. On the ceiling is *Stories of Iphigeneia*, a subject taken from Ovid's *Metamorphosis* and the tragedies of Euripides. It is treated lightly, ironically, with vivid colors. On the walls hang more paintings and an immense, fine tapestry noteworthy for its craftsmanship and shades of color.

Alexander of Russia. But the palazzo did not remain a hotel for long. In 1846 the city government of Florence purchased it for 34,500 scudi (old units of Italian currency), and converted it into city hall. The building erected by Geri degli Spini remained the office building of Florence's

the elimination of superstructures that had been added to the facade by the Da Bagnano family. On January 15, 1881, in the context of an agreement to settle the city's debts, Florence deeded the palazzo—valued at 1,252,000 lire—to the Cassa di Risparmio di Firenze, a banking institution. The Cassa di

city administration for twenty years, until Florence lost its short-lived standing as capital of Italy, and was replaced by Rome. Palazzo Feroni returned to obscurity and was used for a number of different functions. New renovations were undertaken, this time to restore its original appearance, with

Risparmio di Firenze in turn sold it to a certain Ruggero Casardi. Since that time, Palazzo Feroni has increasingly become a commercial building, containing the offices of leading companies, which have successfully settled into the old edifice, fully respecting its remarkable history.

The remarkably fine chapel was originally on the ground floor, where the staircase now stands. Lorenzo Merlini, in the eighteenth century, moved it to the second floor, embellishing it with white-and-gilt stuccoes. The decorations date from the beginning of the seventeenth century, and are the work of

Bernardino Barbatella, known as the Poccetti. We can attribute to his hand the altarpiece with the *Adoration of the Shepherds*, the four Sybils in the corners of the walls, and the barrel vault, upon which is depicted *God the Father in Glory*, surrounded by cherubs and music-making angels.

Palazzo Malenchini Alberti

The entire area between Via dei Benci and Piazza Santa Croce was once occupied by the homes of the Alberti family, Guelphs who came originally from the Casentino area, and arrived in Florence at the turn of the thirteenth century. Many of these houses were demolished by enraged Ghibellines following their victory at the battle of Montaperti, though the ancient tower at the corner of Borgo Santa Croce remains standing.

It was probably as a response to these events that the Alberti family began to purchase land, still on Via dei Benci, but toward the Lungarno (the riverfront avenue), on a line with the Ponte a Rubaconte, a bridge that is now known as the Ponte alle Grazie. By the middle of the fourteenth century, the Alberti family already owned the entire plot of land that is now occupied by the palazzo with its grounds. At that time, however, the palazzo was hemmed in by a welter of densely packed buildings. As for the Alberti family, they clearly exerted considerable influence over every aspect of life in this quarter of Florence. They provided constant support for the

The massive palazzo occupies the corner of the Lungarno and Via dei Benci, not far from the Ponte alle Grazie. The nineteenth-century facade was clearly designed to give the palazzo a fifteenth-century appearance. Along the Arno is the lush vegetation of the garden.

construction of the church of Santa Croce, and Jacopo Alberti made a commitment to erect an oratory on the bridge, in honor of the Madonna delle Grazie (Our Lady of Grace). The bridge received its present name—Ponte alle Grazie—in recognition.

described as a palazzo. It was in fact Giovan Vincenzo Alberti—a count of the Holy Roman Empire and a close acquaintance of both the grand duke Francesco Stefano di Lorena (of the House of Lorraine) and his son Pietro Leopoldo—who arranged to unify the facade and the inte-

The large atrium features corniced vaults and the heraldic crest of the Malenchini family. The atrium was badly damaged during the 1966 flood, and was carefully restored.

Things did not even change very much when the Alberti family was sentenced to exile, due to their rivalry with the triumphant faction of the Albizzi. The Alberti were back in Florence by 1434, with the favor of the Medici, and thereafter their star never really dimmed.

As for their residence on Via dei Benci, at the corner with the Lungarno, it was not until the eighteenth century that it could properly be

rior of the building (1760–63). Giovan Vincenzo's son, Leon Battista, was the last of the Alberti. When he died in 1836, he left the entire estate to a niece, a member of the Mori Ubaldini family. In order to respect a clause in the will that required that the Alberti name be perpetuated, the inheritors became the Alberti Mori Ubaldini family. The new owners immediately set about a number of major renovations: they hired the

The garden, too, has recovered quite well from the flood, though many of the older plants were drowned in the disaster. It was here, in the nineteenth century, that the architect Vittorio Bellini built an "Ionic tepidarium"—a warm sitting room—which has since been converted into residential quarters.

architect Vittorio Bellini to undertake improvements to the interior of the palazzo and in the garden. Bellini built a "tepidarium" (a warm sitting-room in the ancient Roman baths) as well as an elevation with neoclassical columns that contains the garden near the Lungarno. The architect was also commissioned to build an oratory to contain the holy icon that had long been venerated in the chapel on the bridge.

As for the facade, the architect O. Rezzi successfully endowed it with a new, quattrocento-style appearance in 1849. The new facade was spare and elegant, in keeping with the origins of the palazzo itself.

Shortly thereafter, however, the count Arturo Alberti Mori Ubaldini found himself unable to meet his mounting debts. He was forced to sell the family palazzo to another branch of the Alberti family, the Alberti del Giudice. This branch of the family had been residents of France for some time, and had been made dukes of Chaulnes, Luynes, and Chêvreuse. The Alberti del Giudice remained in Florence for only about twenty years. Thus, at the end of the nineteenth century, their palazzo became the property of the marchese Luigi Malenchini, a descendant of the famous Vincenzo Malenchini; for the latter's distinguished service during the Italian Risorgimento, he had been made a Senator of the Kingdom of Italy.

The palazzo's new owners were profoundly affected by two calamitous events during the twentieth century, each of which threatened the structural integrity of the palazzo. First was the destruction of the bridges over the river Arno by the Germans in 1944. Palazzo Malenchini, on a line with the Ponte alle

Grazie, was hit directly by the blast. The second threat was the great flood of the Arno in 1966, when the silty floodwaters swept through the ground floor of the palazzo and devastated the garden and its exotic plants. The garden, the ground floor, and the entire palazzo have since been entirely restored, and the Marchesi Malenchini are still the owners of this palazzo.

The spacious ballroom on the second floor is decorated in gold and white; the walls are frescoed with the sort of architectural subjects that were exceedingly popular in the eighteenth century. Note the refined furniture and the various finishings that are well suited to the whole, giving the room an elegant and lavish appearance.

This majestic staircase lined with splendid tapestries leads to the second floor (below). The two flights of stairs lead to a well-lit access corridor, with two large windows overlooking the garden behind (right). Note the austere, refined style in which the rooms are furnished.

The stone fireplaces that adorn
two halls on the second floor
were installed in the nineteenth
century, during the time of the
dukes of Chaulnes. They come
originally from the Ducal Palace of
Gubbio.

The *salone,* or great hall, on the
second floor; here, the brightly
colored wall coverings, mirrors,
and tapestries are nicely set off by
the large frieze with the light-blue
heraldic crest of the Alberti family,
and by the lacunar ceiling with
rosettes and painted decorations.

Palazzo Davanzati

On the centrally located Via Porta Rossa, midway between the imposing Palazzo Strozzi and the Arno, stands a tall, impressive building. Because of its remarkable architecture and structural characteristics, paradoxically enough, this building has been largely overlooked through the centuries. Its steep narrow staircases; its dark, stern rooms, some more than one story in height; and even the outer structure's sheer vertical height—all these features were sharply at odds with the ideas of comfort and refinement that developed over the ensuing centuries.

This building is Palazzo Davanzati, erected in the fourteenth century by the powerful Davizzi family. A number of members of this family are depicted in the capitals of the columns in the courtyard, and visitors can still admire their features. In 1516, the Davizzi family sold their home to their wealthy neighbors, the Bartolini Salimbeni family; they in turn sold it to Bernardo Davanzati in 1578. The Davanzati family had gained its considerable wealth from trade. Bernardo, who had certainly not neglected the family

The distinctive sandstone facade, with rusticated ashlars on the ground floor, was restored to its original appearance by Elia Volpi. Note the numerous pieces of ironwork punctuating the stone, the three arched doors on the ground floor—a classic fourteenth-century detail—and the *altana,* or covered roof-terrace, added in a later phase to replace the original crenelation.

Below The stone Davanzati family crest, with its distinctive lion rampant, stands out above the second-story windows on the facade renovated by Volpi. Note in particular the interlocking symmetry of the facade's rectangular stone blocks.

Opposite A charming view of the inner courtyard; note the pillars with their octagonal cross-section and up-thrusting arches. In accord with the defensive intentions underlying the entire building, the courtyard is built in such a way that it can be easily guarded against the exterior.

A view of the stairway that leads from the exterior to the upper floors. This is a rare, fourteenth-century structure, with an original construction, supported by large corbels and flying buttresses, part wood and part stone. Note the old coats-of-arms of the Davizzi family.

Below Detail of the stone capital of a column in the courtyard. The small plaque set above it commemorates the knighting of Giuliano Davanzati by Pope Eugene IV.

Above The most unusual capital in the interior courtyard, believed to date from the fourteenth century. It is said that the carved heads are portraits of members of the Davizzi family, the original owners of the palazzo.

interests, had traveled throughout Europe, and had run the family bank in Lyons. He was also a man of learning, however, and particularly loved the classics—he did a celebrated translation of Tacitus, and wrote a number of widely respected treatises.

When Bernardo purchased the palazzo he was almost in his fifties; when he died in 1606, he left it to his children. It remained in the family for more than two centuries.

Beginning in 1772, the Accademia degli Armonici met in the palazzo. This academy had been founded for the encouragement of musical taste. The academicians organized concerts (Luigi Cherubini was a member); they also enjoyed the favor of the grand dukes.

The last Davanzati to own this palazzo was Carlo. Sadly, he ended his own life in 1838 by leaping from the loggia on the top floor. The Davanzati family thus died out, and the building was passed from one owner to another until, in 1904, it was purchased by Elia Volpi, a wealthy antiques dealer who had studied under Stefano Bardini. Volpi's dream was to restore an aristocratic residence of the fourteenth century, down to the tiniest details. Palazzo Davanzati suited his purposes perfectly, and Volpi set to work restoring the building immediately. Volpi's methods may not have been philologically sound; he often resorted to reconstruction or even pure invention. Nevertheless, the result is an

The name of the Sala dei Pappagalli (Parrot Room) on the second floor comes from the odd decoration of the walls, upon which countless parrots were painted, inserted symmetrically among the diamond shapes. This decoration generally imitated fabric patterns (as indicated by the artfully reproduced false folds). At the top, on the other hand, a series of small Gothic hanging arches surmounts an ornamental motif based on trees and birds.

Nail-studded shutters cover the windows, which are quite small, little more than peepholes, and typical of dark fourteenth-century homes. On the monumental fireplace, the central heraldic crest belonged to the Davizzi family; the smaller crest on the left, on a blue field, was that of the Alberti family; and the crest on the right, on a white field, belonged to the Ridolfi family. Probably used as a dining room, this is an exceedingly rare example of an original, painted fourteenth-century room.

outstanding piece of work. The facade was restored to its original appearance, with the three great basket arches on the ground floor (in the fifteenth century, these opened onto three wool workshops), the five symmetrical windows of the second, third, and fourth floors, the many projecting pieces of wrought iron (for tying horses, to support torches and banners, to hold the staffs on which cloths were suspended or ornamental fabrics fluttered on feast days), and the great upper loggia with its jutting eaves.

Inside, walls and partitions that had been built over the course of the centuries were torn down; the more recent whitewashings were wiped away. Once again, the original features were restored to their pristine splendor: the staircase on flying buttresses; the great halls on the second and third floors, with their exquisite Gothic fireplaces and frescoed walls (often painted so as to seem upholstered in fabrics and drapes)—and above the fourth floor, the majestic covered loggia.

The painstaking restorations were completed in 1910, and Volpi decided to crown the work with a refined set of furnishings in the original style, and in some cases dating from the period concerned.

The newly restored Palazzo Davanzati quickly became the object of much public admiration; it attracted illustrious visitors, including the King of Italy. Such a great

The Sala dei Pavoni (Peacock Room) is a bedroom on the second floor, named after the peacocks painted among the wall decorations that are symmetrically divided into little Gothic arches. Each arch contains a coat-of-arms of a family with blood or marriage ties to the Davizzi. Here, too, the walls are frescoed in imitation of fabric.

undertaking may have been the source of enormous personal satisfaction, but it was the undoing of Volpi's financial standing; quite soon (beginning in 1911) he was forced to sell much of the exquisite furniture at auction. In the end, in 1924, he sadly decided to sell the palazzo to the antiques dealer Benguiat of New York.

Benguiat, with his brother Leopoldo, did nothing more than install Gothic windows and Eastern-style columns in the cellars; they left Volpi's masterwork virtually intact (save for the furnishings sold at auction).

In 1951, the palazzo was once again put on the market; the Italian state purchased it, and in 1956 opened it to the public as the Museo della Casa Fiorentina Antica (Museum of the Early Florentine Home). This museum is unique, and it preserves the exquisite and priceless work of Elia Volpi. It gives us a rare opportunity to take a look into the hidden folds of the distant past.

Opposite The Camera Nuziale (nuptial chamber) is the most distinctive room on the third floor of the palazzo. This room is said to have been decorated and frescoed to celebrate the wedding of Francesco di Tommaso Davizzi and Caterina Alberti, which took place in 1359. The fireplace in the corner is situated to provide heat primarily to the section of the room where people spent most of their time. Also, note the frieze at the top of the wall, which describes the lengthy love story of the Chastelaine de Vergi.
Left The concatenated pattern of the wall decorations is quite distinctive; even more noteworthy is the small wooden statue of a lady, set in a niche that is cut into the wall in a sort of three-dimensional trompe-l'oeil.

The great period of the Medici

Palazzo Strozzi; detail of the facade.

Palazzo Strozzi

Directly in the heart of Florence, near the modern Piazza della Repubblica which once held the teeming Mercato Vecchio (Old Marketplace), and along the elegant Via Tornabuoni (which was called Via dei Legnaiuoli, or Street of Carpenters, until the nineteenth century), stands a palazzo that was created through the powerful determination of one wealthy and greatly respected merchant, Filippo Strozzi. Palazzo Strozzi is a majestic and enormous structure, a fitting monument to a man of impact and presence.

In the second half of the fifteenth century, Strozzi systematically began to purchase—from the previous owners, who had names such as Tornaquinci, Popoleschi, and Rucellai—the houses, towers, courtyards, and lands surrounding the rectangular plot of land upon which he had decided to build his own palazzo.

Once he had completed this preliminary step, he turned his attention to a respected architect, Benedetto da Maiano. He entrusted Maiano with the task of building a palazzo that would outshine the prestigious residences built over the

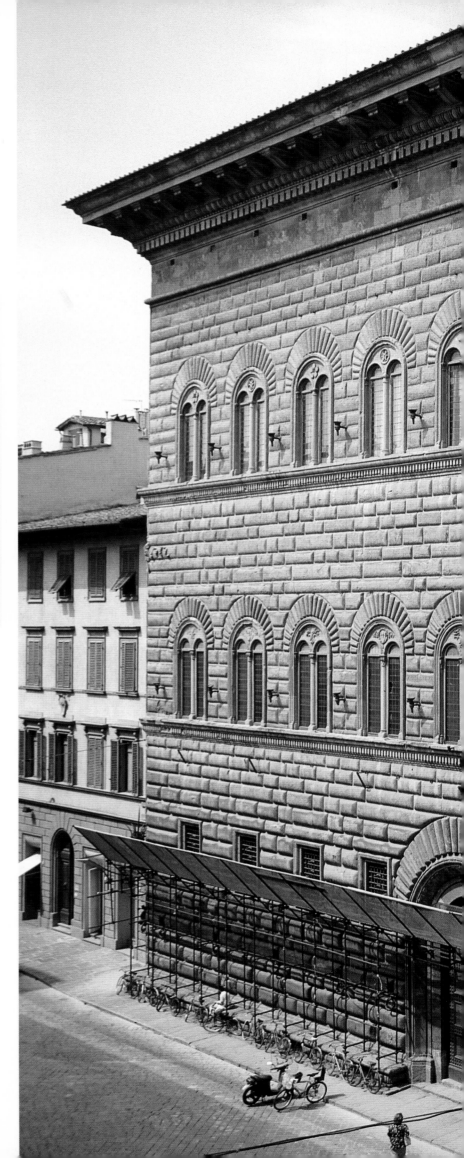

On the powerful facade at the corner of Piazza Strozzi and Via Strozzi, one can clearly see the cornice by the Cronaca, left halfway finished. Also, note the solid portal, which still features distinctive (and very old) nail studs (above).

recent decades by the Medici, Pitti, and Rucellai families.

In 1488, Benedetto da Maiano drew up plans for a building covering a rectangular surface, divided into two symmetrical parts for separate use by Filippo Strozzi's two sons. Work actually began on July 4, 1489, and at roughly the same time, the architect Maiano, who was to have supervised construction, left for Naples.

Strozzi decided to turn to Giuliano da Sangallo; this architect quickly fashioned a wooden model of his proposal for the new Palazzo Strozzi. In time, that little wooden model became famous, but there and then it failed to sway the demanding merchant, who promptly turned to yet a third architect, Simone del Pollaiolo, known as the Cronaca. And it was the Cronaca who finally succeeded in grasping and seconding the aims and ambitions of Filippo Strozzi. He developed a building with unusually tall, sheer stories; a courtyard that seemed to soar upward; a light and skillfully balanced facade (despite the symmetrical and dense texture of the rustication); and exceedingly elegant twin-light mullioned windows, each of which was crowned by an unusually tall crest of ashlars—just as the palazzo itself was crowned by an elaborate cornice that jutted far out over the street.

Under the supervision of the Cronaca, work started up again with great energy, beginning with the wing

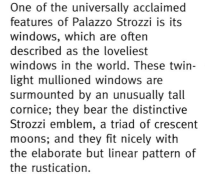

One of the universally acclaimed features of Palazzo Strozzi is its windows, which are often described as the loveliest windows in the world. These twin-light mullioned windows are surmounted by an unusually tall cornice; they bear the distinctive Strozzi emblem, a triad of crescent moons; and they fit nicely with the elaborate but linear pattern of the rustication.

The facade overlooking Piazza Strozzi presents a harmonious composition, punctuated by rectangular ashlars, with cornicework separating each floor, and with the monumental cornice surmounting all. It is the masterpiece of the Cronaca, and the section that remains original was completed in 1502, amid myriad technical difficulties, given its enormous size. The windows were all releaded in the twentieth-century restoration.

overlooking Via Tornabuoni. Within a couple of years, the ground floor was practically complete. Suddenly, on May 14, 1491, Filippo Strozzi died. The palazzo, or what existed of it, was thus passed down to the sons of the merchant. By then, however, there were three of them: Alfonso, born from Filippo's first marriage, who inherited the wing on Via Tornabuoni; and two small boys, Lorenzo and Giovanbattista (the latter was just two years old, and was known to one and all as Filippo when he grew up), born from their father's second marriage. These two late-comers were to inherit the part of the building that faced Via Strozzi and the little adjoining square (Piazzetta Strozzi). But Filippo Strozzi's will was quite strict on one point: his sons could inherit only if they continued the construction of Palazzo Strozzi.

The palazzo continued to grow: in 1495 the second floor was completed, three years later the third floor was finished, and by 1503, the courtyard too could be admired in all its elegance.

As early as 1502 the massive cornice had been completed, but only over the section of the building owned by the two younger brothers. Alfonso, caught up in intricate political machinations, was short on funds; in fact, his part of Palazzo Strozzi never was capped with its intended cornice.

When Alfonso died in 1534, without heirs, his estate

The tall courtyard was also designed and built by the Cronaca. Completed in 1503, and featuring cornicework, oculi, and loggias, it was partly made of *pietra serena*, as was the facade. *Pietra serena* is a troublesome type of stone, in that it is damaged and made particularly fragile by atmospheric agents. Much of the merit for the fine appearance of the palazzo is due to the restorations undertaken from 1938 onward by the Istituto Nazionale delle Assicurazioni. Much of the original stone structure was replaced with new elements, taken from the same quarries used in the late fifteenth century.

passed to his two half-brothers; it seemed that Palazzo Strozzi finally belonged to a unified estate. Not for long, however. Just two years later, in 1536, the young Filippo (Giovanbattista), who openly opposed Medici rule, was sent into exile, and his property was confiscated by the state. Things went better for Lorenzo, who had been less outspoken; still, Lorenzo was forced to halt the decoration underway under the supervision of Baccio d'Agnolo. It was not until 1568 that the grand duke Cosimo I restored—to Filippo's son Lorenzo, by then a cardinal, and to Leone, the son of the exiled Lorenzo—the part of the palazzo that had been confiscated. Thus, the building once again become the rightful property of the Strozzi family, and it regained its place in Florentine public life, with memorable parties and receptions held in its halls. There was no further construction, however, of any note. In 1652, during a meeting of a learned society called the Accademia della Crusca, the entire grand-ducal family stayed as guests of the Strozzi—Ferdinand II, with his brothers Giovan Carlo, Mattias, and Leopoldo. Despite this signal honor, the palazzo soon afterward fell into a period of relative obscurity, following the transfer of the Strozzi family to Rome.

It was not until the mid-nineteenth century, when Prince Ferdinando Strozzi made his definitive return to

Views of the courtyard clearly show the upward thrust in design and construction. The upward thrust is imparted by the stone cornices, as well as by the height of the windows that enclose the little second-floor loggia. The half-circle cornices above the windows are a clear reference to the cornices on the facade. Note the extreme elegance of the capitals with their stylized foliation.

Florence with his wife Antonietta Centurione Scotto of Genoa, that Palazzo Strozzi once again became the center of an intense social whirl.

Its renewed social standing was entirely due to the Princess Antonietta, who was the leading hostess of Florentine high society. The elder of her sons, the prince Piero, commissioned the architect Pietro Berti to build an elegant apartment in the rooms of the second floor. This apartment was entirely conceived and furnished like a sixteenth-century home, and had a fine ballroom, an armory, and a library. It was frescoed by Augusto Burchi. In the same period, Piero's wife, the wealthy Polish princess Sophia Branika, had several rooms decorated in Liberty, the Italian equivalent of art-nouveau. There she held elegant receptions.

Little survives of all that splendor. Piero died childless in 1907 and left the building to the state. There were no children, but there were rightful heirs, and they withdrew Piero's donation, selling much of the furniture and artwork to pay the inheritance taxes. The palazzo remained in the family until 1937, when it was sold to the Istituto Nazionale delle Assicurazioni, an insurance company, which completely restored it.

Palazzo Strozzi now houses such prestigious scholarly institutes as the Gabinetto Scientifico Letterario G.P. Vieusseux and the Istituto di Studi sul Rinascimento.

One of the most interesting rooms on the ground floor is without a doubt the Sala Ferri, a large hall with a vaulted ceiling, used for conferences and conventions by the Gabinetto Scientifico Letterario G.P. Vieusseux, which has a renowned library in the adjoining rooms.

Palazzo Antinori

In Florence, one palazzo in particular can rightly be held up as the paragon of the fifteenth-century palazzo built as the residence of a wealthy merchant. This is Palazzo Antinori, with its austere elegance, unostentatious appearance, well composed dimensions and geometric patterns, and painstaking detailing, which stands at one end of Via Tornabuoni, facing a church that was originally called San Michele Berteldi, and is now named San Gaetano.

As early as 1461, Giovanni di Bono Boni, a leading member of the Arte del Cambio (Guild of the Moneychangers), had purchased a number of houses from a certain Messer Lionardo Bordoni; Giovanni had those houses demolished, in order to build his own house. Construction dragged on for many years; it was still underway in 1466, when Giovanni died, still in his prime. It was Giovanni's father who oversaw the last stages of building, and the palazzo was completed in 1469. Giovanni's father also arranged to sell the newly built palazzo on July 11, 1475 to none other than Lorenzo the Magnificent. No documents survive to tell us the

The facade of Palazzo Antinori dominates the piazzetta of the same name, at the end of Via Tornabuoni. The geometric design and the regular courses of stone emphasize the harmony of the proportions and composition, giving the whole building an elegant, linear appearance. At the center is a stone escutcheon of the Antinori family; there is another coat-of-arms in glazed terra-cotta in the courtyard. Another interesting feature is the stone *panca di via*, or streetside bench; in the fifteenth century this was a standard feature in aristocratic palazzi, and a fundamental component of social life. Very few of them survive.

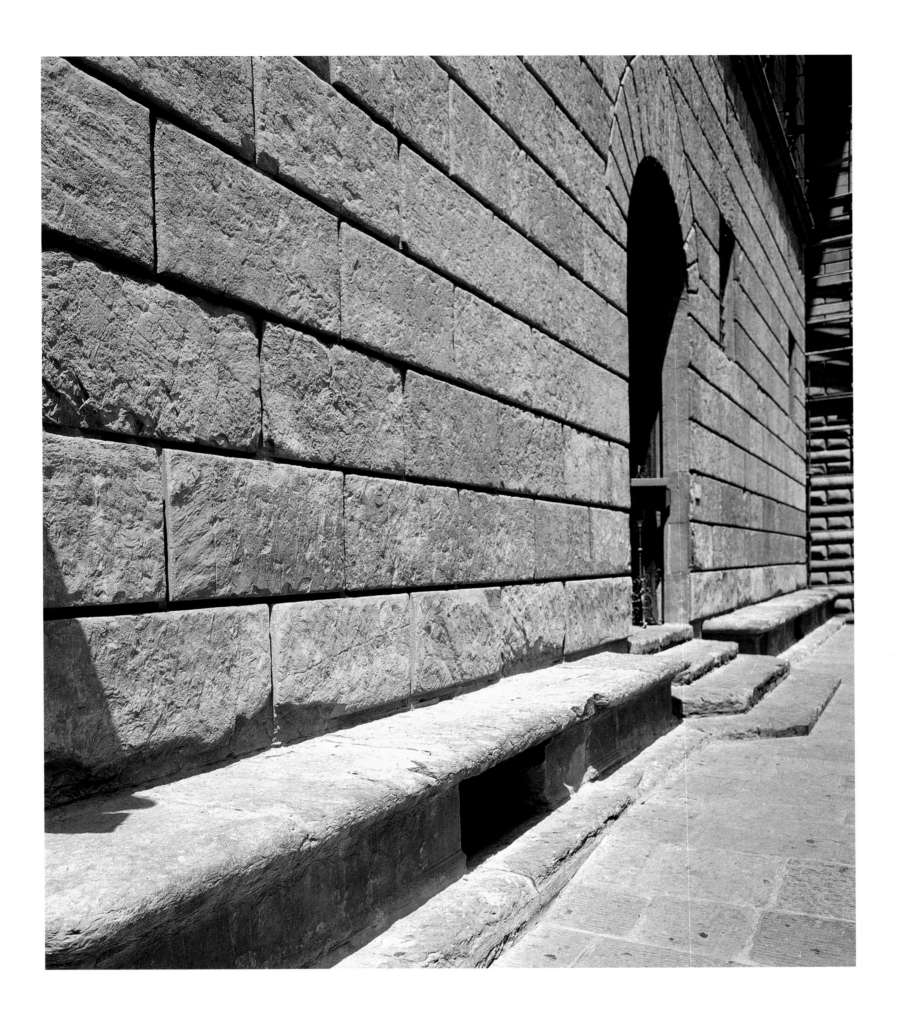

name of the architect who built the palazzo, but a number of clues indicate that it was probably Giuliano da Maiano.

Just a month after purchasing the palazzo, Lorenzo de' Medici sold the new property to two close friends, Carlo and Ugolino Martelli; in 1506 they in turn sold it to Niccolò di Tommaso Antinori, a merchant and a member of one of the greatest noble families of Florence. For centuries the Antinori family had lived in the quarter of Santo Spirito. Niccolò Antinori became the first member of the family to live outside of that quarter; with him came his three sons, Alessandro, Camillo, and Giovanbattista Antinori. Only Alessandro and Camillo, however, were made heirs to their father's trading company and palazzo upon his death; the third son, Giovanbattista, had given clear signs of an erratic, violent character.

Alessandro became a senator and married into the Tornabuoni family. He took it upon himself to purchase and tear down several houses adjacent to his palazzo; he then had the building enlarged, until it attained its present size, bounded by Piazza Antinori, Via delle Belle Donne, and Via del Trebbio. It was almost certainly during this renovation that the garden was laid out and that the rear elevation overlooking it was renovated. This elevation was to undergo further renovation in later years (in particular, note the

The handsome courtyard has three porticoed sides. The well (above, left) is a customary presence, and was vital to everyday life. Note the lovely tall capitals of the five columns, with stylized foliation. The corbels that support the lunettes are typical of the Renaissance style.

The lush garden occupies a narrow space eked out among the surrounding lanes by Alessandro Allori during the sixteenth century. A map by Stefano Bonsignori dating from that period clearly shows a small green space on the present site of the garden.

four *inginocchiate* windows on the ground floor). During this first renovation, however, the facade was certainly modeled by the expert hand of Baccio d'Agnolo. One clear indication of Baccio's presence is the door leading into the garden. It is remarkably similar to another door in a similar son, Vincenzio Antinori, who married a woman from the Capponi family (Teresa Capponi), was another. Teresa Capponi was a well-read and charming woman, who made the palazzo into a welcoming haven for literati and illustrious foreigners; she also made it the site of renowned parties

On the third floor of the palazzo is the elegant apartment of the present-day owners. In particular, note the handsome gallery that runs all the way around the courtyard, nicely lit by the large windows. The rooms house exquisite antique furniture, valuable tapestries, old paintings, a large painted Strozzi family tree, and classical-style statues, including a notable Hermes (below).

location in Palazzo Bartolini Salimbeni, which was certainly built by Baccio. It is known, moreover, that Baccio was in close contact with the Antinori family during this period.

The branch of the Antinori family that descended from Alessandro has maintained ownership of the fifteenth-century residence, right up to the present day. Among the notables in this branch of the family, there have been several senators: Niccolò di Vincenzio Antinori was one; his and receptions (the most memorable social event held in the palazzo remains the great ball of 1752; among the guests were the princes Esterházy of Galantha, and the regents of Tuscany, the princes of Craon). Then there was Niccolò Gaetano Antinori; his son Vincenzo was orphaned at age three. Vincenzo was raised by excellent guardians, who made him a learned man and a lover of the arts, devoted to scientific and mathematical studies. In time he became

the director of the Gabinetto Fisico-Naturale (Cabinet of Nature and Physics, later to become a proper museum, now known as the Museo della Specola). He was also made a member of the editorial staff, for his scientific expertise, of the *Vocabolario della Crusca*, Italy's great national dictionary. And he was selected by the grand duke Leopoldo II as a tutor for the ducal children.

Following the unification of Italy and the exile of the Lorraine dynasty, Vincenzo Antinori, who had never allowed himself to be dragged into politics, took refuge in retirement, surrounded by the numerous family that still looks down upon us from a painting by Giuseppe Bezzuoli, hanging in a corridor on the third floor of the palazzo.

His descendants have undertaken structural restorations of their prestigious home on more than one occasion. The most recent restoration was quite substantial; it was carried out under the supervision of architect Emilio Dori. Following the move of the British Institute and the British Consulate—which had long occupied the second floor of the palazzo—to new quarters, Dori and his workers restored the general silhouette, the roofs and ceilings, and various original structures. The restoration was an admirable success.

The third floor is elegantly furnished, and is used as a swank reception area; the ground floor has been converted into a renowned *cantinetta*, or wine cellar, where visitors can sample the excellent wines produced by the Antinori vineyards.

Clearly, the Antinori family has managed to combine, in a tasteful and measured fashion, respect for a heritage linked to age-old traditions,

and some of the family's modern-day business. It is only appropriate for the building to be right at the heart of these worldly things, elevating them with its noble history and magnificent architecture.

Above On the third floor is a comfortable little living room with a handsome fireplace. Note the wooden fifteenth-century ceiling, with carved brackets, and the wooden shutters on the windows. *Opposite* A large study, also on the third floor, holds a notable collection of books and other publications lining two walls. The room's most remarkable feature must certainly be the fine paintings hanging there.

Palazzo Venturi Ginori

The palazzo's main facade overlooking Via della Scala still features a badly eroded heraldic crest of the Rucellai family and a Della Robbia *Madonna*. On the courtyard facade is a three-arch loggia at the first-floor level; in the early years of the palazzo there was a corresponding loggia on the ground floor as well. The rear facade overlooks the garden (below).

To speak of this palazzo in terms that are chronologically correct, we must begin with the garden, or better, from the ancient *orto*, the Latin *hortus*. In 1482 a sister of Lorenzo the Magnificent, Nannina, was married to Bernardo di Messer Giovanni Rucellai, thus acquiring all the lands in the surrounding area.

The area in question was marshland watered by the nearby river Mugnone (which now runs farther north); for this reason, it was called the Pantano—quagmire or bog. For centuries, landholdings here belonged to the Donati, Acciaiuoli, and Gianfigliazzi families, as well as numerous other illustrious clans. In 1186, a leprosarium, or leper's hospital, was built here; at the end of the fifteenth century, it was the only building that stood in this entire area.

For the first twenty years of his ownership, Bernardo Rucellai simply farmed the land, as had been done before him, raising vegetables and fruit in the Orti Oricellari, as they were called (from a Latinized version of the name Rucellai). Then, toward the end of the fifteenth century, Bernardo decided to have a *casino* built there, a pastoral party house for the Rucellai family, designed by Leon Battista Alberti. Bernardo later had the building and gardens adorned with busts, statues, and ancient sarcophagi. At the corner of Via della Scala and Via degli Orti Oricellari stood a handsome Della Robbia *Madonna*.

Bernardo had special ties with the Medici family, and

Beginning in the sixteenth century, the garden was embellished with fountains, statues, and ancient obelisks, all of which had been painstakingly collected by the Rucellai family. The garden was given a total overhaul in the middle of the seventeenth century by Antonio Novelli, who had been commissioned to do the job by Giovan Carlo de' Medici. Novelli did the giant statue of *Cyclops* (1650), which once stood at the center of a fountain. Built of bricks and stucco, the statue rests its weight on the legs, but also on the cloth drapery and the stick angled behind it. The present-day garden is far smaller than the original one because of the progressive dismantling of the estate.

for many years he welcomed to his Casino all members of the Accademia delle Arti e delle Scienze (Academy of Arts and Sciences)—Niccolò Machiavelli, Luigi Alamanni, Giovanni Cavalcanti, Giovanni Corsini—who enjoyed the patronage and encouragement of the Medici.

When Bernardo Rucellai died in 1514, the Palazzo degli Orti Oricellari was inherited by his two sons, Giovanni (who died in 1525) and Palla. When Palla was forced into exile in 1527, in conjunction with the expulsion of the Medici from Florence, the palazzo and its grounds were ransacked and devastated. When the family returned to Florence, they remained owners of the Casino until 1573, when it was sold to Bianca Cappello, the mistress of the grand duke Francesco I. Upon her death, the new grand duke Ferdinand I made a gift of the Casino to Don Antonio de' Medici, who in turn rented it to the ambassador of the Venetian Republic.

In 1608 the Casino became the property of Giannantonio Orsini, and it remained in the Orsini family until 1640, when it returned to the Medici family, becoming the home of the cardinal Giovan Carlo de' Medici. This cardinal was the brother of the grand duke Ferdinand II; he had the palazzo decorated with series of frescoes by Pietro Berrettini da Cortona and Angelo Michele Colonna. The cardinal then moved his precious gallery of

From the time of the cardinal Giovan Carlo de' Medici up to the fairly recent past, the halls and rooms of the palazzo have been frescoed repeatedly. It began in the seventeenth century with Pietro Berrettini da Cortona and Angiolo Michele Colonna; the process concluded in the nineteenth and twentieth centuries with refined stuccoes and exquisite polychrome decorations. This column-lined hallway offers a perfect example: the mythological figure of Diana, both as lunar deity and as goddess of the hunt (below), "clashes" with the winged figure in the lunette (above), which is clearly a Roman Catholic reference.

One of the most interesting creations of Antonio Novelli is surely the Grotto of Polyphemus, which lies beneath the palazzo, encrusted with sponges and seashells. In it are decorations bearing the heraldic attributes of the Medici family.

paintings there, with works by Raphael, Tintoretto, Titian, and Filippo Lippi. Finally he commissioned Antonio Novelli to build the fountains in the garden, the Cavern of Polyphemus, and a colossal statue of Polyphemus (Cyclops), made of brick and stucco, but so highly polished as to seem like marble.

When the cardinal died in 1663, the grand duke was forced to sell the Casino in order to liquidate his debts, and it was purchased by the marchese Ferdinando Ridolfi, who hired Pier Francesco Silvani to enlarge the residence. The Casino remained in the Ridolfi family until 1765, when it came by inheritance into the hands of Giuseppe Stiozzi. Stiozzi decided to build a Romantic, English-style garden with the assistance of the count and architect Luigi de Cambray-Digny. The Casino changed ownership again, passing from the Stiozzi family to Princess Olga Orloff in 1861. Under her ownership, the architect Giuseppe Poggi restored the building to its original appearance, while the main hall was decorated by Leopoldo Costoli with medallions depicting all the leading thinkers of the time. At the end of the nineteenth century, the building and the garden became possessions of the marchese Ippolito Venturi Ginori, then were inherited by his son Roberto, who died in 1965. The Casino is now the main office of the Florence branch of the Cassa di Risparmio di Pisa.

This excellent work by Pietro Berrettini da Cortona is an *Allegory of Tranquility* (1640–1642), located in one of the ground-floor rooms.

LARVE IMPORTVNE
E SOGNI SPAVENTOSI

Palazzo Rucellai

The facade of Palazzo Rucellai (designed by Leon Battista Alberti, and notable for its flat-arch portals, large corniced windows, flat rustication, and the large stone escutcheons of the Rucellai family) overlooks Via della Vigna Nuova. The large loggia set before the palazzo is commonly believed to have been designed by Alberti.

With the construction of the Palazzo Medici (now Palazzo Medici Riccardi) on Via Larga (now Via Cavour), civil architecture in the city of Florence took a radical new direction. In this context, one of the first and most significant developments was certainly the palazzo built on Via della Vigna Nuova at the behest of Giovanni Rucellai, a respected merchant and renowned patron of the arts. Although he was the son-in-law of Palla Strozzi, who had shown himself to be a bitter rival of the Medici, Rucellai succeeded in maintaining friendly relations with the burgeoning new dynasty; he even succeeded in building a fortune for his own family.

Around 1450 he asked the architect Leon Battista Alberti to build him a fitting home. The result is a palazzo with an unusual facade in which elements from Roman antiquity (the socle with a rhomboid pattern, the small square windows, the symmetrically stacked architectural orders) blend perfectly with decidedly more modern features (the high twin-light mullioned windows on the two top floors, the flat rustication). The supervising architect was in all likelihood Bernardo Rossellino. At first, plans had called for a facade with five vertical bays with a central door, but the number of vertical bays of windows was increased to seven; and a new portal was built, establishing a new if imperfect symmetry.

Giovanni Rucellai had two sons, Pandolfo, the elder, and Bernardo, who was born in 1448. It was on the occasion of the very prestigious wedding of Bernardo and one of the sisters of Lorenzo the Magnificent, Lucrezia de' Medici, known as Nannina, in June of 1446, that the palazzo had its house-warming, as it were. Decked out for the gala, the palazzo overlooked a stage occupying the entire *piazzetta*, adorned with flowers and compositions in fruit. There was dancing and banqueting for three days.

Across from his new palazzo, Rucellai also erected an elegant loggia with three arches, punctuated by tall pillars, which was probably also designed by Leon Battista Alberti. This loggia, in keeping with the customs of the time, was used for the haggling and accounting of business and trade, as well as for private meetings and family celebrations. Over the centuries, this loggia was enclosed—transformed into a closed room that served in the seventeenth century as the studio of the renowned sculptor Giovanni Battista Foggini—and opened again more than once; it is now enclosed by large plate-glass windows that do not hide the structure, and is an ideal exhibition space.

The descendants of Giovanni Rucellai still live in the palazzo. That family has included humanists, senators, historians, and a member of the Accademia Colombaria, who allowed the prestigious

Opposite As a result of the recent renovations, the remarkable large ballroom is now the first room that one encounters upon entering the apartments on the *piano nobile*. Note the little marble stairways leading up to each window.

Left The drawing room on the second floor presents unassuming, yet elegant furnishings, dominated by the large mirror surrounded by a stucco cornice. The ceiling, framed with a monochromatic frieze, was frescoed in the mid-eighteenth century by Gian Domenico Ferretti. The fresco depicts *Olympus*, with Jove, Juno, Venus, Mercury, Ceres, and Hercules (the two latter are clearly visible in the detail above).

institution to hold its meetings in the palazzo.

In the middle of the eighteenth century, Giuseppe Rucellai used his wedding to Teresa dei Pazzi as an opportunity to greatly embellish the entire *piano nobile,* or main upper floor. Worthy of note in these rooms are the frescoes, primarily by Gian Domenico Ferretti.

More renovations and restorations were completed throughout the nineteenth century and in the early twentieth century; of particular significance was the lengthening of the main staircase, which had originally reached up only as high as the *piano nobile.* The third floor, in fact, had originally been intended as a storage area and servants' quarters. It was only later that residential apartments were installed on that floor.

At the turn of the twentieth century, the second floor was the residence of Count Giulio Rucellai and the Countess Lysin, widow of the Prince Woronzow; they were well known for their frequent and spectacular parties. On the third floor lived Count Cosimo Rucellai and his wife, Edith Bronson, an American by birth. She and Cosimo were the forebears of the current owners of the palazzo. Still higher up, above the cornice and practically invisible from the street, is a loggia with a balustrade where there was once an open garden. Later, enclosed and given a dropped ceiling, it became an inhabitable suite, and it still crowns this unusual palazzo.

Also on the second floor is a spacious bedroom whose walls are entirely decorated with trompe-l'oeil architecture. On the ceiling—which is frescoed with mythological themes (the Arts)— note the scrolls showing elevations of the church of Santa Maria Novella (opposite). Giovanni Rucellai took an active part in the completion of that facade under the supervision of Leon Battista Alberti.

Right A painting depicts the classic layout of the early kitchens in this aristocratic palazzo.

Two more excellent features of Palazzo Rucellai: ceilings in which perspectival expertise is bound up with classical subjects (above); and the gallery (opposite), painted in 1756 by Gian Domenico Ferretti, who applied his frescoes of mythological and allegorical subjects to the architecture of Pietro Anderlini.

Palazzo Della Gherardesca

In the fifteenth century a man born into the family of a lowly miller in Colle Val d'Elsa traveled to Florence, and there succeeded in rising through the ranks, attaining a remarkable series of honors until he became the secretary of the Florentine Republic in 1468, and Gonfalonier of Justice in 1486. This man, Bartolommeo Scala, became the target of much criticism from eminent citizens. Although it was probably his rapid rise and his determined personality that drew the attacks, he was specifically accused of having used public funds to build himself a palazzo near the city walls.

The chain of events that led to his accusation began in 1472, when Lorenzo de' Medici ordered Scala to draw up a legal bill of confiscation for the lands and possessions of religious orders around the city walls. These religious landholdings were hindering the much-needed expansion of Florence. As a result of the confiscations, much of this land was deeded to private citizens. Among the land was a plot near the gate of Porta a Pinti, at the end of the Borgo Pinti; Bartolommeo Scala purchased this plot of land from the Spedale degli Innocenti,

Overlooking Borgo Pinti is the eighteenth-century facade built by the architect Antonio Ferri. Note the vertical alignment of portal, balcony, and a French window, topped by the heraldic crest of the Della Gherardesca family.

This vast garden, long cultivated
as a vegetable garden, was
renovated and transformed by
Count Guido Alberto Della
Gherardesca in the nineteenth
century, in keeping with the
Romantic fashion of the time.

or foundling hospital. In 1480 a palazzo already stood on this land, and Bartolommeo Scala lived in it with his family.

The architect who had been hired to build it was certainly Giuliano da Sangallo. Based on the few existing buildings, Giuliano da Sangallo had created a home suspended between city and countryside, open to the surrounding greenery, a long and exceedingly well-lit palazzo. One particularly noteworthy feature is the courtyard, elegantly embroidered with stucco bas-reliefs. It is also bedecked with porticoes with broad arches, and side walls that are low enough to allow a generous amount of daylight to reach the interior.

The Scala family handed down the palazzo and its grounds from father to son for about a century. Finally, Giulio Scala, whose offspring included three daughters (all withdrew to nunneries) and no sons, arranged for the girls to sell the building and adjacent grounds to Alessandro Cardinal de' Medici upon his own death. And that is precisely what happened in 1585.

The new owner wasted no time in renovating and embellishing the palazzo. Frescoes were painted in the halls, ornaments and decorations were installed in the courtyard, and special attention was devoted to the chapel on the ground floor (here, the architect Giovanni Stradano, or Jan Van der Straet, worked in 1586 and 1587). When the new owner became pope in 1605, with

the name of Leo XI, he left Florence permanently for Rome. The former cardinal made a gift of the palazzo to his sister, Costanza, the wife of Ugo Della Gherardesca. The Della Gherardesca family was an old family of counts of Donoratico, and had deep roots and feudal possessions

The marble statues and structures in the garden were designed by illustrious artists in the nineteenth century, including Giuseppe Cacialli, Antonio Martini, and Ottavio Giovannozzi.

along the Tyrrhenian coast, between Pisa and the Maremma; the family did not settle in Florence until the mid-sixteenth century.

The Della Gherardesca family gave its name to the palazzo in Borgo Pinti, and was responsible for the palazzo's present-day appearance. In fact, around 1720, another count Ugo Della Gherardesca ordered major renovations. The entire palazzo was radically altered,

and only the courtyard preserved its fifteenth-century appearance. The facades overlooking the street and the garden were rebuilt, and given a uniform style by the architect Antonio Ferri. Ferri added a number of windows on the ground floor (originally there had only been two), and rebuilt the original loggia. He added two massive forward wings on either side of the loggia. The large portal—surmounted by a balcony and coat-of-arms—was also added in the eighteenth century, as were the frescoes and stuccoes in the halls and gallery on the second floor (done by Alessandro Geri).

The modifications of the garden date from the nineteenth century. Until then, only the area directly behind the palazzo could be described as a garden; the rest of the grounds were planted with vegetable gardens and fruit orchards. It was the count Guido Alberto Della Gherardesca who decided, around 1820, to create a single Romantic-style garden, in accordance with the tastes of the time. This garden was dotted with small Ionic and Doric temples, was crisscrossed by artistically modeled paths and meadows, and was punctuated with statues and copses. The entire project was overseen by Giuseppe Cacialli, Antonio Martini, and Ottavio Giovannozzi.

Fifty years later, another Della Gherardesca, the count Ugolino, was faced with the demolition of Florence's city walls, and the construction of

The work of Giuliano da Sangallo, the courtyard is a true gem. The walls are decorated with twelve large stucco bas-reliefs with classical and mythological themes, and the porticoes (below), with their lacunar barrel-vaults are ornamented using a rather unusual technique. Note the large rosette decoration (left), framed to fit in with the other decorations on the cross-vaults. Originally, the fact that the courtyard was not very deep improved the external lighting. Now a skylight encloses the courtyard to protect the interior.

the new Viale Principe Amedeo, a broad avenue that ran right along the northern side of the garden. He therefore hired the architect Giuseppe Poggi to design and build the monumental gate and the buildings that still enclose the garden on the northern side.

The heirs of count Ugolino sold the estate to Ismail Pasha, the former viceroy of Egypt. In turn, Ismail Pasha sold the estate to the Società delle Strade Ferrate Meridionali, a public works agency. In 1940 the estate was acquired by its present owner, the Società Metallurgica Italian, an industrial corporation. SMI has done considerable restoration of the courtyard and the rooms on the ground floor and second floor; these rooms, with the lush adjoining gardens, constitute one of the most spectacular and interesting architectural complexes in Florence.

The central *salone* of the *piano nobile* is especially majestic. The decoration of the walls and ceiling dates from the eighteenth century, and includes three large paintings framed by stucco cornices as well as six oval paintings above the doors. The three paintings depict notable events in the history of the Della Gherardesca family, and are by Gian Domenico Ferretti, Vincenzo Meucci, and Gaddo Soderini. The detail (left) is from the painting by Soderini, and depicts Gaddo Della Gherardesca being called to govern Pisa in 1330. The globe is by Vincenzo Coronelli.

Palazzo Gondi

Few visitors know that the sloping ground at the foot of the Palazzo Vecchio, along Via della Ninna and Via dei Gondi, is an indication of the tiers of seats of the ancient Roman theater buried beneath; all subsequent construction has been forced to take this underlying slope into account. Among the buildings in question is the palazzo overlooking Piazza San Firenze, built at the end of the fifteenth century by Giuliano da Sangallo, on behalf of Giuliano di Lionardo Gondi. This latter individal was a merchant who had made a fortune trading in Naples; there he had also won the esteem and benevolence of the king, Ferdinand of Aragon. And so, when Gondi decided to return to his native Florence, the new king Alfonso, son of Ferdinand, made Gondi a duke.

In Naples, Gondi had made the acquaintance of Giuliano Da Sangallo, who was working there on behalf of the court of Aragon. Gondi summoned Da Sangallo in 1489 when he decided to build a palazzo that would be a fitting residence for his own family. The Gondi family owned many houses in the quarter of Santa Maria Novella; many of their

The palazzo that stands at the corner of Via dei Gondi and Piazza San Firenze is now much larger than it was when first built; the present version was completed in the second half of the nineteenth century by Giuseppe Poggi. Before Poggi's work, the facade overlooking Via dei Gondi was not unified, and there were only six vertical bays of windows on the side overlooking Piazza San Firenze. The heraldic crest of the Gondi family stands out from the corner of the palazzo. Above the eaves there is an airy loggia with a panoramic view.

storehouses, however, were located in the quarter of Santa Croce. Here, the new duke Giuliano purchased a number of new houses from the city government, from the Arti, and from the Giugni family; he demolished these buildings and leveled an area on which to build his new home.

The palazzo he built was smaller than the one we now see. With six vertical bays of windows on two stories, it possessed two doors, one of them set in the first vertical bay on the right, the other in the fourth vertical bay. We know from the will of Duke Giuliano Gondi, who died in 1501, that he had already taken up residence in the palazzo with his family, but that construction was not finished. The heirs, in fact, still had to oversee and pay for the completion of the palazzo. We do not know what the final stages in construction involved. Some think that the palazzo had yet to be extended toward Palazzo Vecchio, so as to incorporate the other buildings that the Gondi family already owned in the area. Others theorize that the palazzo had to be extended, but in the opposite direction, toward Via Condotta, by the addition of three vertical bays of windows, to give the distinctly asymmetrical doors a central location. In any case, the extension of the palazzo was never completed. The most notable feature of the facade was the intricate motif and texture of the rustication. Also greatly admired was the balconied terrace that

The apartment of the owners is now on the fourth floor, from which there is a stupendous close-up view of Palazzo Vecchio.

The regular rustication was conceived by Giuliano da Sangallo, and was preserved and perpetuated by Poggi. The square windows on the ground floor provided ventilation and light for the storerooms and other facilities.

The little loggia set on the roof dates back quite early in the history of the palazzo, but has been rebuilt a number of times. It offers a view of the entire stunning cityscape of Florence. From here, the tower and crenelated ramparts of the Bargello appear very close, and the dome of Santa Maria del Fiore can be glimpsed through the small, arched window.

surmounted the palazzo, replacing the cornice. Most of all, however, attention focused on the stupendous courtyard, one of Da Sangallo's greatest creations. The courtyard is perfectly geometrical and linear; its crowning touch is the handsome staircase, embellished with exquisitely cut stone bas-reliefs.

Between the sixteenth and seventeenth centuries the prestige of the Gondi family grew, both in Florence and elsewhere. Many family members were made senators; others moved to France and were made dukes of Retz; these emigrants helped their Florentine relatives establish solid contacts in Paris. Some Florentine Gondis were sent to Paris as ambassadors. If the family reputation flourished and grew, the palazzo remained static and unchanged. The sole exception was the lovely fountain installed in the courtyard in 1652 by another Giuliano Gondi, as a *perfezionamento*, a crowning touch. A significant new development came about in 1686, however, when the property was inherited by the two sons of Amerigo Gondi, Vincenzio and Angelo. These two sons summoned the architect Antonio Ferri and asked him to renovate the entire portion of the palazzo located behind the courtyard. This led to the construction of the stables and a series of rooms—nicely decorated and frescoed by fashionable artists, from Matteo Bonechi to Lorenzo del Moro—that

The courtyard of Palazzo Gondi is tall and sober, with oculi, corniced windows, and a top floor marked with stone finishing (opposite). It is unquestionably one of the masterpieces of Giuliano da Sangallo. Connecting the courtyard with the *piano nobile* is an unusual, beautifully composed stairway. The intaglio ornamentation, which extends up onto the ceiling of the stairway, and the stylized ornamentation on the capitals of the columns in stairway and courtyard also act as ties connecting the two spaces.

included a splendid bedroom, where Angelo brought his new bride, Elisabetta Cerretani.

Two centuries passed before further major structural changes were made in the palazzo. In 1870, in the midst of the general renovation of the historic center of Florence, the decision was made to widen the exceedingly narrow Via dei Gondi, alongside the Palazzo Vecchio; the few small buildings that the family owned in this area were confiscated and demolished. The marchese Eugenio Gondi took this opportunity to have the architect Giuseppe Poggi fulfill the last wishes of his ancestor Giuliano Gondi by completing the palazzo. Poggi brilliantly resolved the challenge by adding a vertical bay of windows on the south side of the facade. In so doing he added a door, and thus restored a sense of symmetry to the entire building. He also completed a facade with five vertical bays of windows and three doors overlooking the Via dei Gondi. He used stone from the quarries of Monteripaldi and Altomena that fit particularly well with the stone that had been used by Giuliano Da Sangallo. He built a stone staircase that led from the porte cochere directly up to the *piano nobile.* These changes gave the palazzo its present-day appearance.

After Poggi, only the architect Emilio Dori in the twentieth century did any further renovation; he adapted the rooms on the second and third floors for use as offices and studios. The residence of the owners was installed on the fourth floor, which was originally intended as a storage area and attic; it had a splendid little loggia, to which were added a number of terraces, which still make the cozy apartment one of the most panoramic homes in all of Florence.

Stone decorations and ornamentation, featuring either grotesque figures or the classical plant motif, are recurring elements in the various rooms of the palazzo.

Opposite In the great hall on the second floor, which is no longer inhabited, there is a majestic sixteenth-century fireplace adorned with a large bas-relief. The relief depicts the court of the sea-god Neptune, and is flanked by two slender columns adorned with figures in relief and heraldic crests of the Gondi family and other families linked to them by blood or marriage.

Palazzo Ximenes da Sangallo

Giuliano and Antonio Giamberti were two respected architects in late-fifteenth-century Florence; they are remembered by their working names as Giuliano and Antonio da Sangallo. Around 1490, they began to purchase plots of land along the street of Borgo Pinti. According to the census of the Florentine Republic, Giuliano had already built a house on that land as early as 1498. Rather than speaking of a house—or *casa*—in the narrow sense of the term, however, we should probably refer to a palazzo, given that by the year 1510 Vasari says the building was widely renowned for the paintings that hung in its halls and rooms (among them were paintings by Botticelli and Paolo Uccello), and for the Roman antiquities that were on display throughout.

In 1603 the descendants of Giuliano's son, Francesco da Sangallo, sold the *casa* to Sebastian di Tommaso Ximenes de Aragona, scion of a family of Castilian and Portuguese origin; he had made his fortune in Lisbon through a thriving trading concern he had set up there. Tommaso came to Florence in the early seventeenth century, with his brothers Ferdinando and

There are many original elements in this palazzo, owned by the Ximenes and Panciatichi families, whose heraldic crests appear united (above) to greet all visitors to the building. This palazzo, which was owned by the Da Sangallo family even before the Ximenes family, has always been renowned for its artwork, such as the three classical-style statues that stand before the windows leading from the courtyard into the garden. In the center is Hercules killing the Nemean lion, above is Apollo, and below, Diana the Huntress.

The rear facade overlooking the garden (below) has a glassed-in loggia on the ground floor that corresponds to the loggia in the courtyard. The facade preserves very little of the original appearance, which has disappeared beneath the additions of Silvani, first, and later the renovations ordered by Panciatichi. A stairway leads into the apartments (left).

Emanuele, and soon managed to secure the title of Lord of the town of Saturnia. He was also made senator and, most important, won his way into the favor of the grand duke. It came as little surprise then that his son Sebastiano won the hand of Caterina, the daughter of Raffaello de' Medici, from the branch of the Marchesi di Castellina. Sebastiano, in order to further cement his well consolidated social standing, decided to purchase the palazzo of the Da Sangallo family. Again, it was not surprising that, once Sebastiano had purchased the palazzo, he consulted an acclaimed architect, Gherardo Silvani, and asked him to enlarge the building and renovate the facade. Small traces of Silvani's work can still be seen in the central vertical bay of the main facade, and in the five windows that are symmetrically arranged there, on several stories.

With the passage of the decades and the succession of a series of members of the Ximenes de Aragona family as owners of the palazzo, the halls on the *piano nobile* were embellished and decorated, culminating in the elegant ornaments of the renowned ball room.

Among the illustrious guests who stayed in this refined home, let us mention one in particular, the young general Napoleon Bonaparte. In June of 1796 Bonaparte had been invited to Florence by the resident minister of the French Republic who worked and lived out of a suite of rooms on the *piano nobile* of Palazzo

There are many remarkable rooms on the *piano nobile*, including the Salottino Rosso (Red Parlor) whose elegant wallpaper sets off a lavishly colored ceiling with floral decorations and charming little scene paintings.

Opposite This little room with portrait gallery is lit by a small skylight.

Ximenes. Here the future emperor spent the night in a comfortable bed chamber, waiting to be received by the grand duke.

In the nineteenth century, the line of male descendants of the Ximenes de Aragona family died out, and the family home, handed down through the female descendants, passed through many different hands. In 1816, the last male Ximenes, Ferdinando, left it in his will to the sons of his sister, Bandino and Pietro Leopoldo Panciatichi. This family only owned the palazzo for a few decades, but that was long enough for Maria Anna Paoluccci Panciatichi to create a notable garden, with well tended groves of trees, and have one of the facades overlooking the adjacent park redone in full seventeenth-century style. Maria Anna Paoluccci Panciatichi was also responsible for having much of the palazzo enlarged and rebuilt, while the size of the grounds was reduced by the new road running nearby, the Via Giusti.

At the end of the nineteenth century, the property was inherited by the counts of San Giorgio, and a few years later, by the counts of Arrigoni degli Oddi. Thus, when the countess Oddina married Prince Francesco Ruffo di Scilla, the palazzo formed part of her dowry.

Their descendants and heirs still live in the venerable mansion, in the lovely and well furnished rooms of the *piano nobile*, with a rich and renowned gallery of paintings.

Left The large hall has painted panels simulating a frieze at the top of the walls, and an understated ceiling.
Below A richly frescoed alcove bedroom in typical eighteenth-century style, where the young general Napoleon Bonaparte slept in 1796.
Opposite The vast hall with its light-colored wallpaper and refined furnishings, is crowned by a majestic ceiling with elaborate monochromatic decorations, punctuated by lively little paintings. In the center of the ceiling three small putti take flight against a bright-blue sky.

The vast frescoed ceiling with its mythological subject, done in the eighteenth century, and the heraldic crests of the Panciatichi family dominate the large dining room. The room is also embellished with monochromatic faux architectural decorations. This is a clear example of the painstaking restorations done by the Ximenes de Aragona family during the eighteenth century.

Palazzo Cocchi

Much of the charm of Palazzo Cocchi lies in its remarkable facade, made up of different elements and shapes dating from different periods. The corbel brackets on either side support the extension of the facade. The medieval ironwork was used for hitching horses. The rustication comes from the houses of the Peruzzi family, which once stood here. The windows are set in a framework of arches, cornices, and pilasters.

The central window was transformed in the early eighteenth century into a full-length combination window and door, with a little balcony. From here, it is possible to watch the ceremonies and celebrations held in Piazza Santa Croce.

Directly across from the basilica of Santa Croce—on the site of an ancient Roman theater which is reflected in the layout of many streets in the area—once stood most of the houses that belonged to the Peruzzi family in the thirteenth and fourteenth centuries. Some of those houses were purchased later in the fifteenth century by the Cocchi Donati family, who wished to build their own palazzo on the site. Some scholars believe that they hired the architect Baccio d'Agnolo to design and build their palazzo. Others believe the attribution is inaccurate because civic records may date the construction to the years between 1470 and 1480, and Baccio was born in 1462. There is no doubt, however, that the facade of Palazzo Cocchi has always generated heated debate and curiosity among artists and scholars, because of its singular form and appearance. The facade clearly incorporates features of an existing fourteenth-century building that was subsumed in the new palazzo (in particular, on the ground floor, note the projections and ashlars). The most interesting aspects of the building, however, are to be found on the upper floors, which juxtapose a series of geometric patterns with architectural features such as the flattened pilaster strips, cornicework, arches, windows with or without architraves, and twin-light mullioned windows. Each of these elements stands independently, and yet

The sandstone stairway (opposite) was built at the end of the eighteenth century by the engineer Gaetano Bercigli, so that a small loggia was created on each floor, and the stairwell itself was open and spacious. The vaults covering each landing on the staircase were frescoed in the same period, probably by Giuseppe Collignon. One of these frescoes depicts Arno/Winter, behind which the Florentine Marzocco (lion) looks out, as well as Selene and Ganimede (details).

together they form a whole that is oddly harmonious.

The extremely geometrical composition has led some to propose Giuliano da Sangallo as the architect, when he was newly returned from Rome, where he had been studying classical architecture. Plausible though this may be, and though clear similarities with other work by the great architect seem to support it, it remains a hypothesis.

The Cocchi Donati family had been particularly respected during the Florentine Republic, and had ties with the Da Fortuna and the Sangalletti families. They maintained ownership of the palazzo until the second half of the eighteenth century, when the last descendent of the family, Maddalena, wife of the marchese Ottavio Orazio Pucci, died. Her daughter, Lucrezia, brought the palazzo as her dowry when she married a Serristori, and the Serristori family owned it throughout the nineteenth century. During these centuries, no changes were made in the building's structure. Only the interior was frescoed, in conformity with the tastes of the eighteenth and nineteenth centuries. These frescoes survive, in part. In 1892 the palazzo—which had become part of the estate of the Della Seta family, in the dowry of Maddalena Serristori, who married the count Andrea Agostini Della Seta—was sold to the city of Florence, which used it as a school building. Only recently has it been adapted for use as a city office building.

At the behest of Piero Cocchi Donati, in 1717 construction began on a little chapel on the ground floor. In the center of the chapel is a fresco entitled *Virgin Mary with the Christ Child, Being Adored by Saint Pius V* (left). The entire pictorial decoration, which is clearly linked to the late-baroque tradition in Florence, is by Dionisio Predellini. Note the complex ornaments made of stucco and gilding (as in the sunburst surrounding the monogram of the Savior [above], with heads of cherubs and putti), the little angels holding flowers on the ceiling (opposite), and the festoons and leaves set amongst the architectural elements on the walls.

Palazzo Capponi delle Rovinate

The escutcheon of the Capponi family, set between two windows on the main floor.

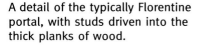

A detail of the typically Florentine portal, with studs driven into the thick planks of wood.

The Capponi family has always been one of the most respected, and largest families in Florence. In every chapter of Florentine history, the Capponi have distinguished themselves, either for the high offices they held (Priori and Gonfalonieri, high public offices, during the Florentine Republic; Senators under the Principality; and cardinals and prelates in every period), or for the great deeds they performed (a classic example is Pier Capponi's fierce resistance to the invading French King Charles VIII). And that is without even mentioning Senator Gino Capponi, who played a major role in the city's nineteenth-century history, prior to and under the new Kingdom of Italy. The Capponi family soon split up into different branches (there were four main branches, but there were also countless subdivisions), and then established ties of marriage with virtually all of the leading families of Florence. It was widely thought in these families that the addition of a Capponi to their ranks through marriage heightened their nobility. As a result the Capponi family had a great many prestigious homes scattered throughout Florence, from Santo Spirito

The facade of the palazzo stretches along the narrow Via de' Bardi. Note the irregular stones, the small windows on the upper floors, which were used for storerooms, and the escutcheon of the Capponi family, set between two older coats-of-arms of the Da Uzzano family.

to San Frediano, from Via Larga (the present-day Via Cavour) to the street that was one day to be known as Via Gino Capponi.

The first palazzo to be inhabited by the Capponi family, however, is the one on Via de' Bardi (still owned by a branch of the Capponi family), conventionally called Palazzo Capponi delle Rovinate because the hill that looms above it has been subject to disastrous landslides (*rovinate*) more than once. Because of the destruction and deaths that ensued, Cosimo I de' Medici decreed around 1550 that it was forbidden to build new houses there. The palazzo is unquestionably quite old, and may date from the turn of the fifteenth century. It was built at the wishes of Niccolò da Uzzano; according to Vasari, the project was entrusted to Lorenzo di Bicci. Although we have no evidence that this attribution is well founded, the palazzo does have a number of interesting and noteworthy features. First of all, let us consider the facade, which is unusual for the rustication seen on the ground floor, which seems to foreshadow much of the work done by Michelozzo and Brunelleschi. There are still marks of the three large projecting openings, typical of fourteenth-century buildings, which were clearly later closed up. That was not the only major work done on the facade: just note the two *inginocchiate* windows and the numerous cornices of the other windows, which do not

hamper the rigorous linear appearance of the facade, embellished symmetrically on either end by two heraldic crests of the Da Uzzano family.

The palazzo has another remarkable aspect: there is a second, radically different facade in the rear, overlook-

ing the Arno. This facade was built by the architect Giuseppe Poggi in the mid-nineteenth century when, in the context of the general renovation and beautification of central Florence, the composite and symmetrical facade overlooking the Arno seemed out of place. With the approval of the two counts—Luigi and Ferdinando—the facade was altered to its

The facade overlooking the Lungarno is sharply different from the facade on Via de' Bardi. Built in the second half of the nineteenth century according to plans by the architect Giuseppe Poggi, this version solved the problems of fragmentation and lack of symmetry that afflicted the earlier facade and blighted its appearance in this prominent location. Note the excellent solution of the side balconies to provide light to the rooms on the second floor.

The courtyard, typical of the late fourteenth century, is at the same time quite innovative. The octagonal pillars support capitals with stylized foliation, with a clear reference to the porticoes and cross-vaults beyond. Note the *graffiti* that extend around the perimeter at the second-floor level.

present form, with two broad side balconies that provide illumination to the rooms within. Another noteworthy feature, ahead of its time, is the courtyard. The fourteenth-century-style *graffiti*, the stylized foliate capitals, the cross vaults, are balanced by the square shape and the broad porticoes, already alluding to fifteenth-century architecture. There are notable rooms on the second floor as well, starting with the enormous *salone*, with four

Right The charming little eighteenth-century chapel holds an exquisite canvas by Pontormo, of the *Virgin Mary with Christ Child.*

Below An odd portrait of Niccolò da Uzzano, the original owner and creator of this palazzo, appears just above a faux-tapestry of two winged figures holding up his coat-of-arms.

windows. This large room has interesting decorations, typically eighteenth-century in technique and subject, featuring landscapes and scenes of battle. Adjoining it are two drawing rooms, the Salotto Rosso and the Salotto Giallo.

Note the remarkable dominant colors (red and yellow) of these rooms, indicated in their names, and present especially in the silk wall coverings (a product of the farms owned by the Capponi family), as well as tastefully

Right, middle All those who enter the palazzo are greeted by this bronze lion. The lion was a symbol of Florentine liberty, and was in heraldic terms an adversary of the eagle, the unmistakable symbol of the Holy Roman Empire.

Right A close-up of the suit of armor (originally dating from the sixteenth century, but in part reconstructed in the nineteenth century) on display in the great hall on the second floor.

Right Dozens and dozens of volumes of the family archive still exist, dating from the fifteenth century. The only part of the archive not present in the palazzo is the purely administrative section held in the Archivio di Stato di Firenze.

The majestic *salone* on the second floor has a coffered ceiling, drapes with heraldic devices, typically nineteenth-century furnishings, and large canvases that may date back to the eighteenth and nineteenth centuries.

selected furniture and accessories in clearly nineteenth-century style.

In the Salotto Giallo there hangs a large, notable collection of paintings, a clear demonstration of the special love the Capponi family has always shown for art. In fact, in the eighteenth-century chapel that opens onto the Salotto Rosso, there hangs a Pontormo Madonna, alongside a beautiful piece of religious stained glass dating from the sixteenth century, a curious collection of relics, and a fresco that is generally thought to date from the time of the Da Uzzano family. In fact, the palazzo was owned by that family for decades, until Agnolo da Uzzano, the son of Niccolò, left the palazzo in the mid-fifteenth century to his cousin Niccolò, the son of Pier Capponi and Dianora da Uzzano. From that time on the building was handed from one branch to another, but it always remained in the same family—that of the Capponi. (It remained the property of the heirs of Niccolò until the seventeenth century, then it was inherited by Ferrante Capponi, a member of a collateral branch, and from him to another line; a member of that line was the other Ferrante, who paid for restorations and frescoes throughout the *piano nobile* in the first half of the eighteenth century.) And the palazzo still belongs to the Capponi family today, who preserve its remarkable architectural, pictorial, and decorative details, as well as its furnishings.

Below An eighteenth-century fresco in which Minerva, the goddess of wisdom, subjugates a lion, the emblem of strength, covers the ceiling of a room that leads to the garden.

The exquisite Salotto Giallo (Yellow Drawing Room) opens off the *salone.* The fine upholstery and wallpaper is made from silk produced on the Capponi family's own farms.

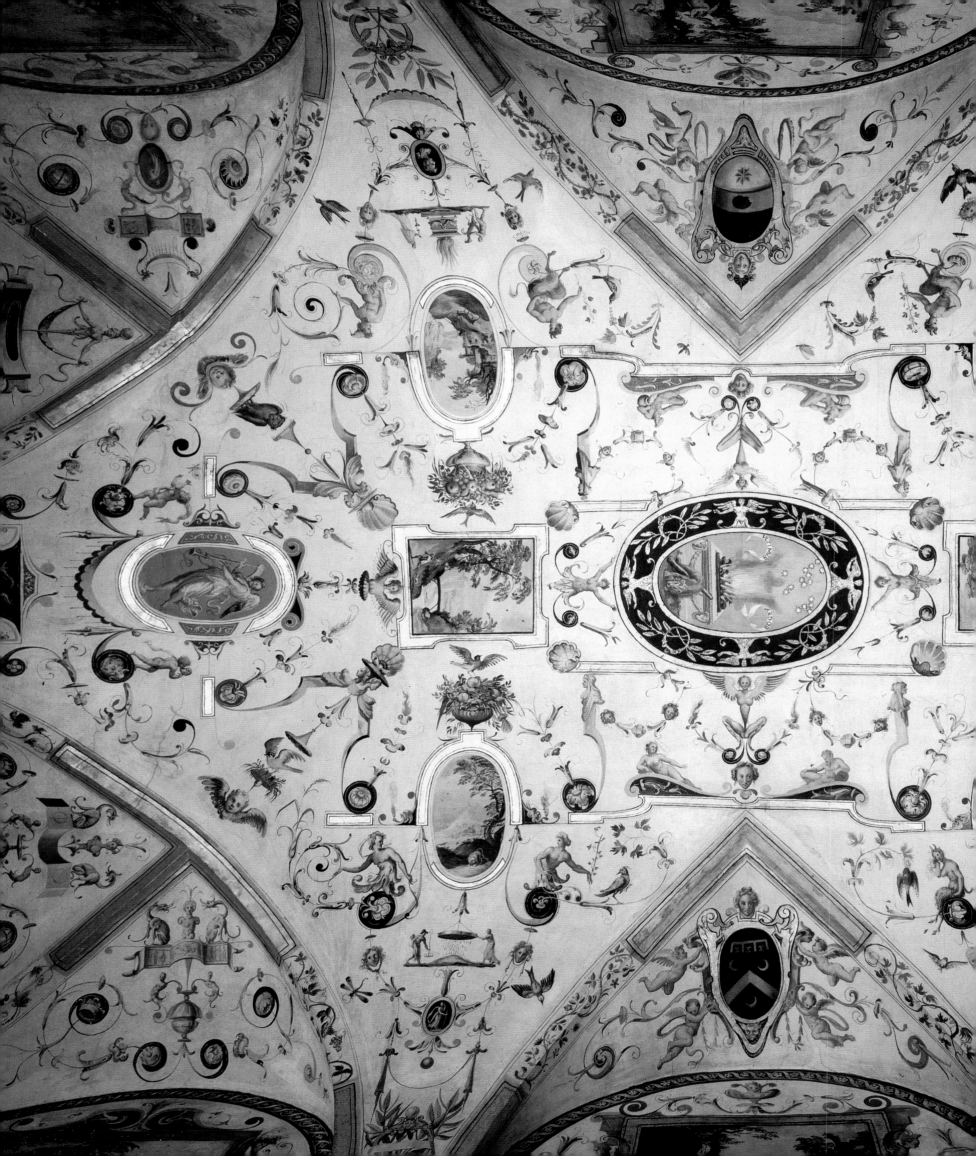

Aristocratic homes in Grand Ducal Florence

Palazzo Portinari Salviati;
decoration by Alessandro Allori
and assistants in the little hall
adjacent to the Cortile degli
Imperatori (Courtyard of the
Emperors).

Casino Torrigiani del Campuccio

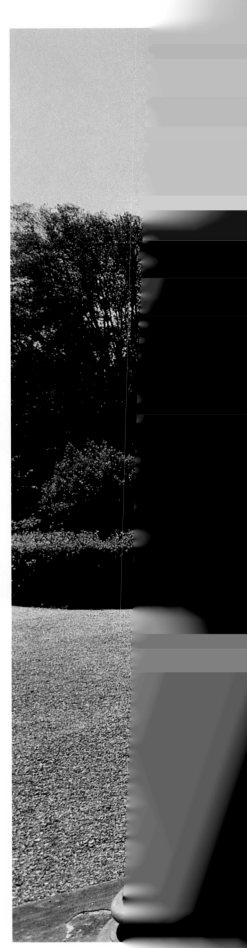

In the crowded quarter of Oltrarno, amidst the dense crisscrossing welter of streets, lanes, and alleys, there lies, unbeknownst to the passerby, one of the largest parks in Florence. Protected on one side by the walls and buildings of Via dei Serragli—the street that for centuries has run, straight as an arrow, to the city gate of Porta Romana—and on the other side by one of the few surviving fragments of the ancient ring of Florence's city walls, this huge garden offers virtually no outward signs of its presence. And yet, when the Torrigiani family purchased their first houses and their first orchards and vegetable gardens on Via del Campuccio, the area was hardly considered a particularly elegant one, or even a residential area at all. Stagnant water rendered the site unhealthy, because adequate drainage and irrigation was lacking. (For that matter, almost all of the land near the city walls in the Oltrarno area had long lain bare of homes and buildings. This land was largely planted with vegetable patches, or it simply lay abandoned; in short, the city authorities had not been encouraged to intervene.) The very air was considered bad as

Two buildings stand out in the garden. There is the nineteenth-century villa (above), which was built on the site of the venerable old Casino dei Del Rosso. A drawing from the nineteenth century shows what the building looked like originally. There is also the villa on Via del Campuccio, built by Bernardo Fallani and renovated by Gaetano Baccani. From its airy portico there is a fine view of the garden and the handsome tower.

The marchese Pietro Torrigiani collected and commissioned a series of statues, as well as Roman sarcophagi and marble urns, and used them to decorate his garden. Among them are life-size statues of Aesculapius and Ceres, by Baldassare Peruzzi, and a vine-dressing putto, by Lorenzo Bartolini. Many of these artworks still adorn the paths and flowerbeds of the garden.

a result, and harmful to one's health. Still, the Torrigiani family was not easily daunted, and they tenaciously pursued their objective: they planned to build an elegant *casino*, a country lodge midway between the open countryside and the crowded city, with a pleasant view of vast stretches of greenery. Here, in accordance with the customs of the period, parties could be organized, leisurely afternoons could be spent, and refuge could be found from the baking summer heat of the city.

Raffaello Torrigiani was the first member of the family to buy property in this area; he purchased two houses and a vegetable plot. His son, Luca Torrigiani, followed Raffaello's example, acquiring other plots of land in the same zone. The family soon undertook reclamation work; work also began on the enlargement and renovation of the existing buildings. And so, by the end of the sixteenth century, a large and aristocratic residence already stood, overlooking Via del Campuccio. Before long the renown of the Orti dei Torrigiani began to spread, establishing a reputation for high-quality farm products. Greater still was the growing reputation of the family home for the parties and festivals that were held in the section of the gardens planted with little groves of cedar and jasmine trees.

Things remained largely the same throughout the rest of the seventeenth century and much of the eighteenth

The careful and detailed nineteenth-century plan (right) shows the vast scope of the renovation and rebuilding of the garden undertaken by Cambray-Digny. The result was a perfect English-style garden, in which large greenhouses were soon installed and used to shelter the tropical plants and botanical rarities for which the Torrigiani estate became famous.

century; the only notable change was a growing specialization in the gardens, with more than a few species of exotic plants of considerable botanical interest.

Finally, in 1777, Luigi Cardinal Torrigiani died, the last male heir to the family property, leaving the entire estate to his little grand-nephew, Pietro Guadagni, the four-year-old son of Teresa Torrigiani. When the little boy had grown, he took his mother's surname, and showed a particular attention to, and interest in the garden, which he soon enlarged. Between 1802 and 1817 he purchased the land just beyond the garden walls. On this land stood, and still stand, the "second walls" built by Cosimo I de' Medici as added fortification for the city. In the same years, Pietro purchased a *casino* from the Del Rosso family, with a long avenue that ran into Via dei Serragli; upon this land was built the villa that stands in the center of the present-day garden. Lastly, he purchased yet another *casino* that also overlooked Via dei Serragli. Thus, in that fifteen-year period, the grounds attained their present size and extension, reaching as far as Porta Romana, and covering ten full hectares.

The architect Luigi Cambray-Digny, later succeeded by Gaetano Baccani, worked to transform the appearance of the estate, creating a perfect Romantic-style garden: three aristocratic homes, avenues, large plazas,

In 1821 Gaetano Baccani had a small lodge torn down to make way for his remarkable tower (*torrione*) which provided a visual mnemonic device of the name and coat-of-arms of the Torrigiani family. Inside the tower, a stairway connects the floors; there is a library, a "cabinet" of astronomic devices, a group of telescopes, and, at the top, a little open terrace.

The second-eldest son of the marchese Pietro Torrigiani, Carlo, wished to create a lasting memorial in the garden to the man who had created it. He commissioned the classical sculptural group (left) by P. Fedi, in which a father advises his young son to follow the right path.

flowerbeds (one of which was particularly large, circular, and was encompassed by a horsetrack; it has always been known as the *Ippodromo*), and a large tower built by Baccani. This tower was meant as a concrete manifestation of the Torrigiani family escutcheon. In it was installed a *gabinetto di macchine astronomiche* (studio of astronomic machinery). Also dotting the estate were little classical temples and even a Grotta di Merlino (Merlin's Grotto). In a short time this became one of the most renowned places in Florence, particularly popular with foreign visitors. When a number of suites in the villas were made available for rental in the nineteenth century, foreign visitors snapped them up. Lady Charlotte Campbell, daughter of a Duke of Argyll; Prince Gustav Vasa, descended from King Vasa of Sweden; and the Count de La Rochefoucauld were all able to admire the vast botanical gardens, tended with zealous care by small armies of gardeners.

Even today, although the garden has been split up due to the technical demands of succession and inheritance among the many branches of the family, the Giardino Torrigiani remains a place of great charm, as well as a working garden with a notable nursery. Indeed, it is quite easy to understand why the son of Marchese Pietro Torrigiani chose to erect a monument to him in the heart of the immense garden that he did so much to nurture and preserve.

The villa on Via del Campuccio dates back to early times: it was a simple country lodge when Raffaello Torrigiani purchased it in 1531. As early as the sixteenth century it was transformed into an aristocratic residence, and was further enlarged in the mid-seventeenth century by Senator Carlo Torrigiani and his wife Camilla Strozzi. Its current appearance dates from the nineteenth century. In front of the building, a large round flowerbed opens out around the large statue of Marchese Pietro Torrigiani.

Palazzo Nonfinito

The houses set at the corner of Via del Proconsolo and Borgo degli Albizzi belonged for many years to the Pazzi family; indeed this street corner was known as the Canto dei Pazzi. It was this same Pazzi family that linked its name to the inglorious and unsuccessful conspiracy against the Medici in 1478. On November 10, 1592, all of the houses were purchased by Alessandro Strozzi, son of the senator Camillo Strozzi; Alessandro had them torn down to make way for his own new palazzo.

He summoned the architect Bernardo Buontalenti, and had him design the ground floor with its distinctive *inginocchiate* windows and the entire *piano nobile*.

Actual construction began on July 15, 1593, and many master craftsmen worked on the building. The cost of the project soon spiraled out of control, and Alessandro Strozzi realized that he could not finance it by himself. He therefore decided to involve his half-brother, Roberto, the son born out of wedlock of Alessandro's father Camillo. Camillo had declared Roberto to be his legitimate son, and sent him to Venice to engage in commerce, and Roberto

Bernardo Buontalenti designed the two facades of Palazzo Nonfinito, including the *inginocchiate* windows on the ground floor and the two portals with small balconies and heraldic crests. He also designed the *piano nobile*. But he never completed the project. Therefore, the facade overlooking Via del Proconsolo was completed by Giovanni Caccini, who worked in particular on the portal (left) and the huge Strozzi coat-of-arms on the corner of the building (above).

The facade overlooking Borgo degli Albizzi was originally meant to be the main facade of the palazzo, and so it was for many years, despite the narrowness of the little street. Notable are the portal by Bernardo Buontalenti—Gherardo Silvani wrote that a portal more handsome has never been seen—the stone escutcheon of the Strozzi family, the little balcony, and the frieze with elegant festoons and grotesque decorations (detail above).

had succeeded brilliantly in his new trade. In 1596 Roberto purchased half of the estate; the following year he purchased the other half, thus becoming sole owner.

Roberto had long resided in the Veneto, and he at first planned to entrust the completion of the project to an architect from that part of Italy: Vincenzo Scamozzi.

The choice did not yield the hoped-for results, and soon Tuscan architects were again supervising construction. Giovanni Caccini completed the facades and the portal that opened onto Via del Proconsolo; he also created the large coat-of-arms that can be seen high over the corner of the two streets. Vignola worked on the part of the second floor that overlooks Via del Proconsolo. Ludovico Cardi, known as the Cigoli, built the courtyard. Santi di Tito da Sansepolcro was responsible for the monumental staircase, clearly influenced by similar structures built by Vasari.

The work of so many illustrious architects, however, led to steadily rising costs, and once again the owner was faced with what seems to have been a recurring situation in the history of this palazzo: Roberto Strozzi ran out of money and was forced to suspend construction. As a result, parts of the courtyard and the mezzanine above the second floor remained unfinished. Thus the palazzo got its name—Palazzo Nonfinito, the unfinished palazzo.

Various collateral branches

Opposite This elegant courtyard was designed and built by Ludovico Cardi, known as the Cigoli; all the same, the vaguely Palladian proportions, the interplay of lines and arches, columns, and half-columns, have all led scholars to hypothesize the influence or participation of the Vicenza-born architect Vincenzo Scamozzi, if only at the drawing board.

The monumental staircase was built at the beginning of the eighteenth century by Santi di Tito da Sansepolcro. At the foot of the stairway is a colossal wooden statue, property of the Museo Nazionale di Antropologia (National Museum of Anthropology), depicting a Patagonian native. The statue was carved in the second half of the eighteenth century at the behest of the grand duke Pietro Leopoldo, on the basis of an account by an English ship captain named John Byron, who had just returned from a voyage around the world. According to Byron's account, the tallest inhabitant of Patagonia that he had met stood eight feet tall.

of the Strozzi family handed this prestigious home down over the generations, without completing construction or beautifying the interior. At last, in 1802, the palazzo was purchased by Giovanni di Francesco Guasti; twelve years later he in turn sold it to the government of Tuscany. It was thus that Palazzo Nonfinito became the headquarters of the Ministry of the Interior and the feared police force under the House of Lorraine. Following the unification of Italy, it housed the Consiglio di Stato (Council of State) during the brief period when Florence was capital of Italy. It then became property of the Italian Postal and Telegraphic Service. Since 1920 it has been the site of the Istituto di Antropologia e Etnologia of the Università di Firenze. This institute was founded in 1869 by Paolo Mantegazza, and has since gained world-class prestige.

On the second floor, where the Museum of Anthropology is now located, there is a little chapel filled with frescoes. Amidst the rich seventeenth-century decorations, exquisite chinoiseries were added in the eighteenth century (above). The floor is made of inlaid marble, and the ceiling features an elegant allegorical scene painted on a gold background (left). Also on this, the *piano nobile,* is a particularly attractive corner room featuring a large fireplace (far left). Above the fireplace is a plaque (opposite), dedicated by the Società Italiana di Antropologia ed Etnologia (Italian Society for Anthropology and Ethnology) to its illustrious president, Giuseppe Genna, a renowned anthropologist of the nineteenth century. The perfectly preserved eighteenth-century ceiling is by Domenico Ferretti.

LA SOCIETÀ ITALIANA DI ANTROPOLOGIA ED ETNOLOGIA
AL SUO GRANDE PRESIDENTE L'INSIGNE ANTROPOLOGO
GIUSEPPE GENNA

Palazzo Bartolini Salimbeni

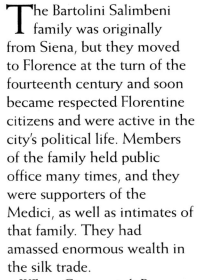

The facade overlooking Piazza Santa Trinita, by Baccio d'Agnolo, was revolutionary in the first half of the sixteenth century due to the pilaster strips, jutting cornices, niches to hold statues, and the massive upper cornice, or *cornicione*. The stone escutcheon with the lion rampant is a symbol of the Bartolini Salimbeni family. Note the handsome crossed windows, surmounted by pediments that are alternately triangular and ellipsoidal. On the cross-bar of the windows appears the family motto, *Per non dormire* (Lest we sleep). Behind the palazzo, the tower of Palazzo Vecchio can be seen in the distance; in front of it stands a monolithic column erected by Cosimo I to commemorate a Florentine victory over Siena. On the column stands a statue of Justice by Francesco del Tadda.

The Bartolini Salimbeni family was originally from Siena, but they moved to Florence at the turn of the fourteenth century and soon became respected Florentine citizens and were active in the city's political life. Members of the family held public office many times, and they were supporters of the Medici, as well as intimates of that family. They had amassed enormous wealth in the silk trade.

When Giovanni di Bartolomeo di Leonardo Bartolini Salimbeni decided to build a palazzo for himself directly across from the church of Santa Trinita, just a stone's throw from Palazzo Feroni, he also decided—good businessman that he was—to keep a ledger of all the expenses and payments, the Libro della Muraglia. The first entry bears the date of February 27, 1519 (this was actually 1520, because the Florentine year began on March 25).

This ledger is a treasure trove of information. It informs us, for instance, that Giovanni Bartolini, as he signed his name, purchased houses and workshops in the area in which he planned to build for the sum of 1,929 florins, and that he then had those buildings torn down. We further know that from the very beginning of construction, the project was entrusted to the respected architect Baccio d'Agnolo, who worked on the project until May 28, 1523, when construction was largely

complete. By this time, total costs amounted to roughly 10,000 florins.

These three years of hard work produced an exceedingly original palazzo; so original, in fact, that a hail of criticism and even harsh attacks poured down upon the architect. The facade in particular prompted much discussion: it was too innovative for its time, with its jutting eaves and stringcourse cornices marking each floor, with its slender columns flanking the portal, with its triangular pediments atop door and windows. Baccio d'Agnolo responded cleverly to the attacks. On the pediment that topped the portal, he carved a Latin inscription that reads: *Carpere promptius quam imitari* (It is easier to criticize than to imitate). In the end, time proved the architect right: his forward-looking approach found numerous fervent imitators in successive decades.

On the facade of the palazzo, specifically on the cross-bars of the windows, another inscription reads: *Per non dormire* (Lest we sleep), the motto of the Bartolini Salimbeni family. This motto refers to a story concerning a member of the family, who, in order to be the first one to market and purchase a shipment of silk at an excellent price, drugged the wine of his closest rivals with opium. Note the unmistakable blooms of opium poppies along the friezes that run the length of the building.

If the facade overlooking

The courtyard of this palazzo is embellished with elegant decorations, including an array of grotesque *graffiti* attributed to Andrea Feltrini that extends up to the third floor. The courtyard has a little side loggia on the second floor, softened by graceful arches and a lacunar ceiling (the photograph on the facing page was taken from the little loggia in question); there is also an earlier loggia on the third floor. It once extended around all four sides, though it has since been sealed up. On the fourth floor is a second full loggia, facing south.

Santa Trinita was the most controversial, the facade on Via Porta Rossa is also worthy of mention. Note the majestic portal, the crossed windows, and the oculi just beneath the eaves. All three different types of stone used in sixteenth-century Florence were employed in the facade: *pietra serena, pietra forte,* and *pietra bigia.* This is a noteworthy and unusual feature.

In spite of the initial harsh criticism of the facade, there was only praise for the elegant courtyard. Originally porticoed on three sides, the courtyard featured a small and finely decorated loggia on the second floor. There was also a loggia on the top floor, surmounted, oddly enough, by a second loggia facing south. *Graffiti* decorations adorned the walls up to the third floor. Also worthy of note is the staircase, with its original stone handrail. The rooms in the top floors are squeezed into the limited space available, within the area bounded by the two streets below.

The Bartolini Salimbeni family lived continuously in this palazzo until 1839, and then rented it out, as was fairly common practice in that period. The palazzo thus became one of the prestigious hotels in Florence, the Hôtel du Nord; among the celebrities who stopped here was the American writer Herman Melville. In 1863, the palazzo was sold to Prince Pius of Savoy, and in ensuing decades sections of the palazzo were sold to the Malvezzi, Sanvitale, Laparelli, and Franzoni families, until the entire estate was purchased by the Marchesi Salina Amorini of Bologna. At one point the palazzo was used as the French consulate. In 1961 it was thoroughly and painstakingly restored, which partly halted the deterioration of the magnificent sixteenth-century facade.

The second loggia, set high up on the roof, was probably added in a later phase of construction; in any case it has a number of typical sixteenth-century features. It opens out on three sides, facing south: from here there is an excellent view of the historical center of Florence.

Opposite The sixteenth-century courtyard at the ground-floor level.

Palazzo Bargellini, formerly Palazzo Da Verrazzano

In the heart of the ancient quarter of Santa Croce, wedged into the dense welter of houses crowded one against another, on the secluded Via delle Pinzochere (the name of the street comes from a convent of Franciscan tertiary nuns that once stood in this quarter), stands a large, austere palazzo, marked by its broad streetside bench. This is the venerable old residence of the Da Verrazzano family. It still has a number of original and interesting features: the bench; the large windows on the two top floors, surrounded by round arches made of flat ashlars; the unusually pronounced, jutting eaves that extend nearly halfway over the street below. The courtyard, too, is quite spectacular. It was originally porticoed symmetrically on two sides, but only the portico nearest the entrance survives, decorated with exquisite capitals topping the columns. From the courtyard, one enters a small but enchanting garden, which, although it has been enlarged over the centuries, can be described as a tiny niche set in a surrounding wreath of buildings, tucked away and hidden amidst the taller structures. One would never guess from outside that the garden is there, despite the magnificent trees that have grown in it for centuries. The staircase that runs up to the *piano nobile*, with its original stone handrail, is also quite remarkable; even more so is the spiral staircase, also made of stone, that runs from the cellar up to

The facade of Palazzo Da Verrazzano features a *panca di via* (streetside bench), windows with cornices made of flat ashlars, sharply jutting eaves, and harmonious overall proportions. There is also a little courtyard, porticoed on one side, and embellished by capitals carved with a plant motif. This courtyard leads directly into the lovely garden. In earlier times, there were two porticoed sides, but the second arcade was sealed up at some point.

the topmost floor of the palazzo.

It is not known with any certainty who designed and built this palazzo. Many scholars have suggested Baccio d'Agnolo but there is no decisive evidence to support this attribution.

What is known for certain is that, before the palazzo was built on this site in the sixteenth century, the fifteenth-century home of one of the most eminent Florentine Humanists, Poggio Bracciolini, stood here. That building, along with other adjoining structures, was later purchased by Giovanni del Zaccheria, who sold the estate in 1505 to Gherardo di Michele Da Cepperello. We can state with some certainty that the family of the latter decided to demolish the existing buildings with a view to constructing a single, large palazzo. If the family did so, it only preserved ownership for a brief time, because by 1578 the estate was already a possession of the Alamanneschi family. The shifts in ownership over the centuries were intricate and tangled, but in 1650 the palazzo was purchased by the Dell'Antella family, and sold just twelve years later to Isabella Gerini, the wife of the senator Andrea Da Verrazzano, a relative of the famed navigator and explorer.

Because the Da Verrazzano family retained ownership longer than any other, the palazzo became generally known as Palazzo Da Verrazzano. When the Da

The halls on the second and third floors have been restored with painstaking care by the Bargellini family. An original fireplace remains in the room (above) adjacent to Piero Bargellini's former study.
Opposite The study has been preserved as it was ever since Bargellini's time as mayor in the 1960s. The handsome paintings and the refined furnishings are perfectly in keeping with the original rooms and structures of the palazzo.

Verrazzano family died out in 1819, however, the palazzo passed into the hands of the Casamorata family, and then the Parenti family.

In the end, the palazzo came into the possession of the Bargellini family, which still owns it and which has preserved and restored it with great devotion. Piero Bargellini, who served as mayor of Florence and was a respected writer, had his study in this building. He did much to preserve the artistic and historical treasures of the city.

And it was in this building that Mayor Bargellini lived though one of the saddest periods of modern Florentine history: the flood of November 4, 1966. The quarter of Santa Croce was one of the hardest hit, and Palazzo Bargellini—flooded five meters deep by the water of the Arno—long bore the signs of this catastrophe in the layers of muck and silt left behind when the water receded. Nowadays, nothing hints at the terrible flood damage, but Florence still remembers the bravery and devotion of Bargellini, the *sindaco dell'alluvione,* the mayor of the flood.

The garden of this palazzo is a genuine oasis, a haven of greenery and coolness carved out among a dense stand of tall houses. It was originally much smaller than it is today (it was square at first, and was enlarged by the purchase of adjoining lots). It now has very old, large trees. One tree in particular, a magnolia, is actually landmarked and protected by the Soprintendenza dei Beni Ambientali as an "environmental resource." And from high above the garden, one can see the distinctive silhouette of the cathedral, flanked by the Torre della Badia and the Torre del Bargello.

Palazzo Giugni

When a merchant attained a certain level of prosperity, it was almost traditional for him to use part of his wealth to build a palazzo for himself, as if to demonstrate his success. Simone da Firenzuola was no exception to this rule. This brother of the noted writer Angelo da Firenzuola purchased a house with a garden on Via Alfani, and then, in 1565, commissioned Bartolomeo Ammannati to tear down the house and replace it with a far more prestigious building. Work must have proceeded quite quickly—in 1577 the new owners were already residing in their palazzo—and the results were worthy of note. In some ways the building showed signs of daring experimentation. Note the portal with its rusticated cornice topped by Doric features, or the elegant simplicity of the windows, in marked contrast with the complexity of the heraldic crest.

Of equal interest is the courtyard, entirely decorated in *pietra serena*, with distinctive independent loggias on the ground floor, and enclosed loggias on the *piano nobile*.

Simone da Firenzuola must have been quite happy with Ammannati's work, at least to

Opposite The rear facade, which overlooks the garden, has a stately poise, especially after the restoration undertaken recently by the engineer Francesco Fraschetti. Note in particular the composition of the central structure, which culminates in the little loggia. A large coat-of-arms above the entrance (hidden by the tree in this photograph) was carved by the Opificio delle Pietre Dure to replace the sixteenth-century original, which has been removed for conservation.

Above The facade overlooking Via Alfani has been described as a masterpiece of the Mannerist period. Bartolomeo Ammannati experimented with a number of sometimes contrasting approaches in his work on this facade (for example, the clash between the very simple windows and the exceedingly elaborate coat-of-arms). The results, however, were always noteworthy and sometimes quite harmonious.
Left The escutcheon of the Giugni family is found on one of the eighteenth-century doors in the gallery.

The courtyard too has many notable features: the arrangement of the cornicework in *pietra serena*, serving as a counterpoint to each arch; the four separate loggias on the ground floor, clipped at the corners by the jutting sections of the rooms inside; and the two loggias on the second floor, enclosed by large windows.

judge from his will, drawn up in 1592. He forbade his two sons, Filippo and Angelo, to sell the palazzo, and enjoined them to pass it down to their own sons. Since Filippo and Angelo both died without heirs, however, the ownership of the estate passed to their sister Virginia, who was married to a certain Vincenzo Giugni. Upon her death in 1640 the palazzo became part of the estate of the Giugni family, one of the oldest and most glorious families in Florence.

Virginia's son, Niccolò Giugni, who was a senator and the marchese of Camporsevoli, established his home in this palazzo. He immediately undertook a number of projects designed to beautify the place, including the friezes that adorn the rooms, and the splendid basin in the garden. His descendants did even more: they enlarged the building, adding a new interior wing, and created a remarkable grotto on the ground floor, designed and built by Lorenzo Migliorini, as well as a fine gallery on the second floor. This gallery was entirely decorated and frescoed; in it hung many excellent paintings, including a great number of Medici family portraits.

The estate remained in the Giugni family until 1830, when it was sold to Count Giovanni Maria della Porta and his wife, Caterina Doria Colonna. They were the first owners to do any substantial restorations. Even greater restorations were undertaken

Left The garden was rearranged and renovated over the course of the seventeenth century. Dating from that period are the various marble decorations and the fountain with a large statue of a giant being overwhelmed by falling boulders.

Opposite The remarkable grotto was completed in the last decade of the seventeenth century by Lorenzo Migliorini, at the behest of Niccolò Maria Giugni. It was built on the ground floor, during a general enlargement of the building. The painstaking and lavish baroque decorations are based on a theme of the seasons.

at the turn of the twentieth century by the Fraschetti family, which still owns this palazzo. The main purpose of the work undertaken was to restore the original size and appearance of the interior, with the elimination of additions that had been made over the years. As an exam-

ple, consider the *salone* on the second floor, which the elimination of two partition walls restored to its original size. More recently, the rear facade, which overlooks the garden, also regained its original austere elegance. Currently, the large rooms on the second floor, with the exquisite gallery, house the Lyceum Fiorentino, a prestigious cultural institution.

The gallery on the second floor was also built at the wishes of Niccolò Maria Giugni, probably in 1691 on the occasion of his wedding to Luisa di Giovanni Giraldi. The decoration of the ceiling was done by Alessandro Gherardini, who painted *The Apotheosis of Art and the Artist*. The walls are adorned with portraits of members of the Medici family and with perfect reproductions of Vasari's paintings in Palazzo Vecchio. Interspersed are excellent stuccoes and busts. On the whole, the room retains its original appearance.

Palazzo Budini Gattai

The portal on Via dei Servi is surmounted by a large, richly decorated window and the stone Grifoni escutcheon (right). The facade overlooking Piazza Santissima Annunziata (top, and opposite) has a raised central vertical bay, designed around the third window in order to maintain symmetry with the other facade. This further accentuates the asymmetrical position of the secondary door. The rear facade has an arcade opening onto the garden (above) and the garden itself features a fountain of Venus, attributed to Giovanni Bandini.

The ancient Palazzo Grifoni, now known as Palazzo Budini Gattai, is considered a major example of the last generation of historic Florentine palazzi—those built from scratch in the second half of the sixteenth century, either for court dignitaries or for the favorites of Cosimo de' Medici and Francesco I de' Medici. Erected some distance from the center of Florence out of considerations of space, these new palazzi were meant to serve specific needs and offer elegant surroundings in which to receive guests. At the same time, they offered an opportunity for trying out new and original architectural solutions and approaches. Such was the case with Palazzo Grifoni, built between 1557 and 1563 for a wealthy court officer, Ugolino di Iacopo Grifoni, Cosimo's secretary and personal favorite, as well as the former butler of Duke Alessandro de' Medici.

Beginning in 1549, Grifoni had purchased a series of houses that once belonged to the Ricci family, set at the corner of Via dei Servi and Piazza della Santissima Annunziata. Eight years later, he entrusted the design and construction of his new palazzo to the most renowned and fashionable architect of the time, Bartolomeo Ammannati, who was paid one hundred ducats for the job. Ammannati, who was building a number of other palazzi during the same period, developed a number of remarkable ideas in his

At the end of the nineteenth century all the rooms on the ground floor and the *piano nobile* were restored and partly rebuilt (especially the halls on the ground floor, which were originally designed as atriums and facilities). The Salotto Rosso (Red Parlor) on the ground floor, and the entrance to the apartment on the second floor are fine examples.

work on Palazzo Grifoni. He built the facades entirely of uncovered brick, a radically new feature in the Florentine architectural landscape, and put large windows on the ground floor, which was quite a change from the projected openings and arcades of fifteenth-century palazzi. Also notable was the way in which he underscored the central vertical bays of both facades. In the facade overlooking Via dei Servi, he used a combination of portal, framed window on the second floor, and family escutcheon. He used the same approach in the facade overlooking the Piazza della Santissima Annunziata, coopting the third window on the ground floor, and thus reducing the importance of the secondary portal standing next to that window, used as a porte cochere. We should also consider Ammannati's refined and painstaking decoration of doors and windows, in perfect harmony with the rest of the facade. Lastly, he incorporated a five-arch interior loggia overlooking the rear garden, lavishly decorated with corbels carved by Ammannati himself. The architect also devoted considerable attention to the garden, perhaps to make up for the lack of an interior courtyard, a constant feature in the typology of the Florentine palazzo. Of particular note is the fountain of Venus, believed by some historians to have been carved by Ammannati himself, though others (specifically Ulrich Middeldorf) believe it to be

A single lower flight of this staircase leads up to two switchback parallel flights, and onto the second floor. Built in 1892 according to plans by Giuseppe Boccini, the staircase is thought to have been completely decorated by Giulio Bargellini.

the work of Giovanni Bandini.

By 1563, Palazzo Grifoni was largely complete, except perhaps for the third floor, which was missing what are now three rooms on the side overlooking the Piazza della Santissima Annunziata, near the Loggiato dei Serviti. This missing portion evidently prompted comments and criticism; nonetheless, it was not until the 1720s that Pietro Gaetano Grifoni decided to complete the third floor, and the facade. Pietro Gaetano Grifoni's wife, Lisabetta di Piero Capponi, renowned for her beauty and her entertaining, brought a period of renown and splendor to the palazzo, following its first one hundred fifty years of relative tranquility. When the Grifoni family died out at the end of the eighteenth century, the palazzo was purchased by Ferdinando Riccardi. He died in 1847, bequeathing the building to the Mannelli family, who in turn sold it to Niccolò Antinori. Finally, his heirs sold the palazzo to Leopoldo Gattai around 1890.

Gattai was the owner, with his son-in-law Francesco Budini, of a major building company, which had received sizable contracts during a great urban renewal of Florence. This consisted of a number of projects undertaken in the wake of Tuscany's annexation to the kingdom of Italy, during which time Florence served as United Italy's capital for a short period. The work made the two men rich, and at the end of the nineteenth century they decided

The refinement and elegance of the furniture and wall coverings—the product of substantial renovations and alterations made at the end of the nineteenth century—are particularly evident in the dining room on the ground floor. Also worthy of note in this room is the nineteenth-century coffered ceiling; its striking impact is due to the fact that it is made of ceramic.

to purchase great amounts of farmland. They also purchased the palazzo on Via dei Servi. As soon as they held deed to this building, they set about restoring it; the architect Giuseppe Boccini decorated the building in the late-nineteenth-century style that still adorns it. In 1892

the monumental staircase was built and lavishly decorated by two artists, Burchi and Bargellini, who were working for Boccini. This staircase leads up to the *piano nobile*, which was also embellished with frescoes, wooden ornamentation, and a cunning blend of period furniture and various decorative arts, which can still be admired there. The floor in a hall on the second floor was painted in oils by the stucco-artist Fercini, who reproduced the pastoral canvases hanging in another hall on the *piano nobile*, executed for the Budini Gattai family by Raffaello Sorbi. The

The powerful hues of the wall coverings dominate the large second-floor Salone Rosso, and are echoed in the various articles of furniture. In the center of the frescoed ceiling, surrounded by a large cornice with abundant decorations, there is an allegory— probably an Allegory of Music— completed at the end of the nineteenth century.

facade too was restored; the *seggetta di via*, a streetside bench, was rebuilt and the friezes, stone window-decorations, and cornices were redone as well.

The palazzo still belongs to the heirs of Leopoldo Gattai and Francesco Budini, who occupy only one wing. The

The majestic Sala dei Bovi on the *piano nobile* overlooks the Piazza della Santissima Annunziata. Its name, roughly "Hall of Oxen," comes from a reproduction on the floor of a number of pastoral paintings by Raffaello Sorbi; the reproductions were done by a master craftsman, G. Fercini, who worked for the Budini Gattai family at the turn of the twentieth

century. The original paintings can still be seen hanging in the second-floor dining room (bottom). The floors were covered with wall-to-wall carpeting when the room became the office of the President of the Regional Council. One can hardly miss the frescoed ceiling (opposite); at its center is an idyllic scene with swans and peacocks.

rest of the building was leased for over twenty years to the Tuscan Regional Government, which used it as the headquarters of the regional council until the end of 1994. The palazzo is now entirely available to the Budini Gattai family.

Palazzo Corsini Suarez

The facade overlooking Via Maggio consists of six vertical bays of windows; the windows on the second and third floors are the oldest. The *inginocchiate* windows on the ground floor and the semi-windows on the top floor were clearly inserted later, by Gherardo Silvani.

In the quarter of Santo Spirito stood the earliest houses of the Corsini family, who arrived in Florence in the mid-twelfth century from the Val di Pesa. This family of hard-working merchants had established a trading company by the year 1300, and possessed considerable wealth. Even the financial downfall of Edward III, the king of England, failed to unhinge this family's great power when many of the great financiers of Florence, including the Bardi and Peruzzi families, who had extended considerable loans to the English monarch, were ruined by his insolvency.

In the fourteenth century, the houses of the Corsini family were clustered on Via Maggio. The largest of these houses belonged to Messer Filippo (1334–1421), brother of the cardinal Pietro. Filippo served as ambassador more than once, but his position of eminence ultimately led to unfortunate consequences. During the uprising of the Ciompi, a revolt against the more powerful families and the domineering rule of the Arti Maggiori, the leading guilds, Filippo's houses were burnt, and almost all were razed to the ground. Filippo was not easily discouraged, however, and when the situation seemed to be under control, he set about rebuilding. The new palazzo that arose was an imposing building in the classical fourteenth-century style, with two rows of ample windows (still present) on the second and third

The heraldic crest of the De Larderel family is preserved in the Archivio Contemporaneo.

Gherardo Silvani also designed the notable carved wooden eaves. They project considerably, with seashells (the Suarez family's particular attribute) and other heraldic decorations beneath.

Inside the secondary entrance on Borgo Tegolaio is this well-lit and austere vestibule with an elegant eighteenth-century fresco on the ceiling. The door to the mezzanine (above, right) is surmounted by a stone ribbon bearing the name of the original owner, Baltasar Suarez; above it is the recurring heraldic attribute, the seashell.

floors. The facade was stern and elegant, and had six vertical bays of windows.

The palazzo was inherited by Filippo's second-born son, Gherardo, and remained the property of Gherardo's descendants until 1559. Over the following thirty years, the palazzo changed owners twice; it was first deeded to Marzio Marzi de' Medici, the bishop of Marsico; then to Matteo Bartoli. In 1590 it was purchased by a Portuguese nobleman, Baltasar Suarez de la Concha, a courtier who was related to the grand duke himself (he was married to the sister of Camilla Martelli, the second wife of Cosimo I). Along with the palazzo, Suarez purchased two adjoining houses located to the rear, on the side running parallel with Via Maggio. He then took great pains to join all three buildings, incorporating them into the single structure of the palazzo. The palazzo thus acquired a second, narrower facade overlooking Borgo Tegolaio. Suarez also enlarged the courtyard, to which decorative capitals and architraves were added.

At the beginning of the seventeenth century, Baltasar's son, Fernando, hired Gherardo Silvani, a noted architect, to make some improvements in the building. Among these improvements was probably the redone ground-floor facade, with the *inginocchiate* windows and a large central portal, and the entire fourth floor, with its slightly smaller windows, and immense jutting eaves, embellished with

The courtyard still has a number of late-fourteenth-century features, such as the distinctive octagonal pillars. Later, more-elaborate architraves and capitals were added with grotesque decorations and stylized foliation (above). The balcony runs around the entire second floor.

carved heraldic motifs. Counterbalancing those eaves on the interior is the immense wooden canopy with carved shells and spheres, which overhangs the courtyard on three sides.

The courtyard is quite interesting in and of itself. Note the balcony that runs around the entire second floor, and the unusual octagonal fourteenth-century pillars. These latter were the source of inspiration for later capitals and columns installed during the ownership of the Suarez family, and feature the Suarez coat-of-arms, along with the Cross of St. Stephen. The Suarez family was endowed with the Baliato di Firenze, the highest ranking title of the Order of the Knights of St. Stephen, and since the palazzo, as part of the family estate, automatically became part of the Baliato di Firenze, it was for many years generally called the Palazzo della Commenda di Firenze.

When the Suarez family died out, the palazzo on Via Maggio became city property, and was used as the headquarters of a branch of the Florentine police force. The first restoration dates from 1918 and was financed by the city of Florence. More thoroughgoing restorations were done in the 1970s, when the city government decided to make the building the headquarters of the Archivio Contemporaneo del Gabinetto Scientifico Letterario G.P. Vieusseux, one of the most respected cultural institutions of Florence, long headed by

One of the most interesting rooms on the piano nobile is the bedroom (left). A typical, richly frescoed eighteenth-century room, it is decorated with stuccoes, and marked by an alcove designed to accommodate the bed. The ceiling frescoes are softened by motifs common in the eighteenth century when agrarian themes prevailed, and seashells, emblems of the Suarez family, are scattered throughout. In this room are two mementos of scholar Giovan Pietro Vieusseux: a marble bust and an early nineteenth-century painting, which depicts him recounting his adventures in Europe to his father, Pietro.

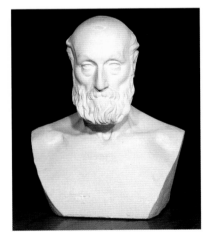

Alessandro Bonsanti, an intellectual and a former mayor, who has lavished care and dedication upon it.

Established in 1979 and opened to the public many years later, the Archivio, a scholarly archive of literature, possesses major collections donated by leading figures of nineteenth- and twentieth-century Italian culture (among them, Giuseppe Montanelli, Emili Cecchi, Angiolo Orvieto, Giuseppe De Robertis, Eugenio Montale, and Alessandro Bonsanti himself). It is now one of the most important cultural centers in the Oltrarno area. In the 1990s, the ground floor became the offices of the Gabinetto di Restauro Librario (Studio for the Restoration of Books), which was an offshoot of the Gabinetto Vieusseux, founded directly following the disastrous flood of 1966. It was founded to rescue the books in the library run by the Gabinetto in Palazzo Strozzi—books that were badly damaged by the mixture of mud and fuel-oil carried by the flood waters. Thousands of volumes have indeed been saved through the work of this virtually unique center, which operated for twenty years in the rooms of the Certosa Cistercense del Galluzzo (Cistercian Charter House). And many more books will be rescued in the future (among them books from the Biblioteca Nazionale Centrale in Florence, Italy's national library) in the new and permanent offices on Via Maggio.

The specialized task of restoring books has been entrusted to the Gabinetto di Restauro Librario of Palazzo Corsini Suarez; it is a job that requires enormous patience, care, and skill, given the desperate state of many of the books damaged in the 1966 flood. The results of such painstaking labor often seem miraculous.

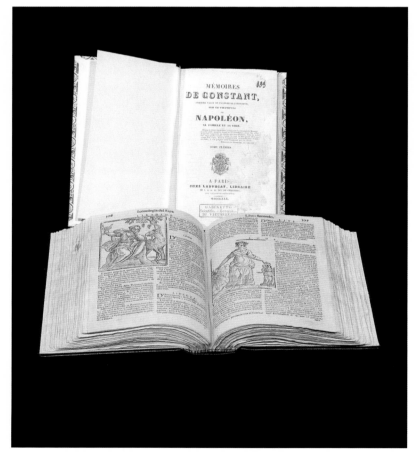

Above On the third floor, a vast hall accommodates the library of Angiolo Orvieto, which was donated to the Archivio Contemporaneo by this noted Florentine intellectual. This library is a perfect reproduction of Orvieto's own library.
Right On the fourth floor is the Sala della Capriata, built in the 1980s by architect Francesco Gurrieri for conferences and lectures.

Palazzo Ricasoli Firidolfi

The imposing facade overlooking Via Maggio, adorned with the heraldic crest of the Ricasoli Firidolfi family, clearly indicates that the *inginocchiate* windows on the ground floor were added after the completion of the rest of the facade. The other windows date from the sixteenth century, and are arranged along six vertical bays. The sixteenth-century courtyard (opposite) with three porticoed sides and one half-vaulted side, is absolutely intact.

One of the chief thoroughfares in the densely inhabited quarter of Oltrarno is Via Maggio. While the name might suggest a reference to the month of May (*maggio*), it is in fact a reference to *Maggiore*, or "largest," because this has long been the quarter's main street. It should therefore come as little surprise that some of the most prestigious and remarkable palazzi in Santo Spirito line this street in particular.

Palazzo Ricasoli Firidolfi was built by the Ridolfi family, not, as the name would suggest, the Ricasoli family. The Ridolfi, at the turn of the sixteenth century, acquired a number of houses on this street, houses which had previously belonged to the Velluti and the Migliori families. Then-senator Giovanni Francesco Ridolfi had those houses demolished in order to build his own palazzo in their place. Around 1530 he took up residence in the new palazzo with his wife, Camilla Pandolfini. The children and descendants of the couple distinguished themselves for their generous commitment to public life and politics, as well as for their love of the arts. Before long, in fact, the palazzo contained a number of fine sculptures and paintings.

When this branch of the family died out in the seventeenth century, however, their entire estate fell into the hands of another Ridolfi branch, descendants of Piero Ridolfi and Contessina de' Medici, one of the daughters

of Lorenzo the Magnificent. It remained in their possession until they sold it to Maria Lucrezia Firidolfi in 1756. Firidolfi was a new surname adopted by a branch of the Ricasoli family, and over the decades, and through a series of marriages, the various lines of this family were reconnected. Lucrezia Firidolfi married Giovanni Francesco Ricasoli Zanchini, then their son Alberto married Elisabetta Ricasoli, the sole heir to Bettino Ricasoli, until the palazzo was rightly given the name of Ricasoli.

Over time the Ricasoli family also established ties with the Corsini and the Rosselli Del Turco families, and they continued to live in their home on Via Maggio until the early decades of the twentieth century. The Ricasoli family certainly rivalled the Ridolfi family's love for culture and the arts. Their library became famous, and their collection of art was equally renowned, featuring paintings by Fra Bartolommeo and Caravaggio. The halls and the *salone* (great hall) had been frescoed in high style during the eighteenth and nineteenth centuries. Of special note was the chapel, which is traditionally said to have been decorated by Giorgio Vasari himself. As for the designer and builder of the palazzo as a whole, the name remains unknown. We do know that the facade originally had no windows on the ground floor. The handsome *inginocchiate* windows were added only in a later phase.

The corbel brackets supporting the lunettes in the courtyard are adorned alternately with the heraldic crest of the Ridolfi and a Saint John the Baptist, patron saint of Giovanni Francesco Ridolfi, the owner of the palazzo.

The suites on the *piano nobile* have often been the site of spectacular receptions and entertainments, and their decoration is therefore particularly notable. The ceiling of the great hall is embellished with fine nineteenth-century frescoes with mythological subjects.

The courtyard, on the other hand, is intact in its original form. It has a simple, soaring elegance, with a stern portico that is softened by exquisite capitals and corbels, decorated with alternating Ridolfi family crests and images of St. John the Baptist, patron saint of the first owner of the palazzo, Giovanni Francesco Ridolfi. Also intact is the steep stairway with stone decoration that leads up to the *piano nobile*, whose entry vestibule also maintains its fifteenth-century appearance and layout.

The profusion of frescoes adorning the halls are based on Biblical and mythological themes, and are clearly eighteenth-century in style. The frescoes in the large *salone*, on the other hand, date from the nineteenth century, and were done by Pietro Rabbajati.

If we can still today admire the features of this palazzo in all their beauty, the credit goes in part to the farsighted initiative of Baron Alberto Ricasoli Firidolfi, who spent heavily in the second half of the nineteenth century to restore the exterior of the palazzo. More recently, restorations have been done, chiefly inside, on the frescoes that adorn the halls. The palazzo is still property of the Ricasoli family, but is now occupied by a dance school.

The ground floor has one particularly charming room, now used by a school of dance. The walls and the ceiling are entirely frescoed in a typically eighteenth-century style. The trompe-l'oeil walls depict architectural structures and classical ruins (opposite) and the elaborate scenes on the ceiling include the liberation of the winds (detail above). The dynamic figures in the foreground and the skillful realization of perspective give the whole room a remarkable appearance.

Palazzo Rosselli Del Turco

One of the few Romanesque churches in Florence, the lovely church of the Santi Apostoli in the little Piazzetta del Limbo, is interesting but relatively little-known. Located along the narrow Borgo Santi Apostoli, the *piazzetta* is so-named because a children's cemetery was once located there. (Catholics believe unbaptized children spend eternity in Limbo.) The little church hardly stands out among the tall buildings that surround it, and it was even more over-shadowed four centuries ago when an impressive, aristo-cratic villa rose by its side.

It was the turn of the six-teenth century, and the Borgherini were a particularly well-to-do family. Because they owned a number of houses along the Borgo Santi Apostoli, directly adjoining the church, they hired the esteemed architect Baccio d'Agnolo to build a palazzo worthy of their high estate. The chief client was Salvi Borgherini, and we know that in 1515 the palazzo must already have been completed, or at least suitable for habita-tion, because in that year Salvi's son Pierfrancesco Borgherini was married to Margherita Acciaiuoli. The

The exceedingly narrow Borgo Santi Apostoli prevents a full appreciation of the facade, which was designed and built by Baccio d'Agnolo, and also hides the size of the palazzo. A better under-standing of its structure can be obtained from the model of the building, done by R. Menchiari in 1992, which is now the property of the owners of the palazzo. *Below, left* This coat-of-arms of the Cavalier Giovanni Del Turco is taken from an old volume in the Archivio Rosselli Del Turco.

Opposite One can see a vertical section of the main facade from the old Orto dei Borgherini across the street; this is the separate garden of the palazzo.

The wrought-iron banner-holder which still attracts curious attention on the corner of the palazzo is probably not authentic. It is in all likelihood a nineteenth-century copy.

dowry of walnut furniture and other objects that her father ordered from Baccio d'Agnolo became legendary. There were chests, chest-benches, headboards, and beds, all finely carved and painted, and all meant to decorate the halls of the palazzo. So great was their fame that, during the siege of Florence in 1530 by the king of France, the Florentine Republic seriously contemplated offering the whole set of furniture to the royal besieger, in hope of placating his wrath. Only Margherita's vociferous protests (Pierfrancesco was in exile at the time) prevented the cowed Florentine government from doing so.

Baccio d'Agnolo had started work on the building in 1507, and was immediately faced with specific obstacles. The nearby church considerably limited the available space, and all decisions had to take the church into account, since the south side of the palazzo joined its perimeter.

One of the first and most notable obstacles was lack of space for a courtyard. Thus, the courtyard was replaced by an atrium directly adjoining the presbytery and apse of the church. From that atrium ran the two-part staircase that led up to the entry foyer on the *piano nobile*. Two more flights of this staircase, which led up to the third floor, have since been partially demolished and rebuilt. In a curious use of materials, the ceiling above the stairway was constructed entirely of stone.

On the second floor is the

The narrow facade overlooking Piazza del Limbo (above)—with its distinctive religious images set in the wall, flanked by plaques (detail opposite)—adjoins the northern side of the ancient church of Santi Apostoli, with its distinctive Romanesque style. The central location of this palazzo is made abundantly clear by the view from the rooftop terrace, including Palazzo Vecchio, Orsanmichele, the Bargello, and the Duomo (opposite, top).

salone, a notably handsome room in which Benedetto da Rovezzano, who had at the time (1505) just returned from France, built an elegant fireplace entirely decorated with bas-reliefs. It is now in the Museo del Bargello. He built another solemn and linear fireplace for an adjoining room, which is thought to be the bedroom of Pierfrancesco and Margherita. The wooden *solai* (ceilings) are also quite interesting—they were built by a team of master woodworkers and specialized craftsmen who worked with Baccio d'Agnolo. This same team also made all of the doors and the nail-studded shutters on the windows. Baccio completed his work with a three-light *altana,* a covered roof-terrace facing south and overlooking the church of Santi Apostoli.

Around 1530 Pierfrancesco Borgherini and his brother Giovanni purchased a number of houses across from the palazzo. They intended to use the land to lay out the garden that was in such fashionable demand at the time, and which could be created in no other way. A small, verdant appendage was thus established, separated from the palazzo itself by the Borgo Santi Apostoli.

The palazzo remained in the Borgherini family until 1749 when Senator Pier Francesco Borgherini was overwhelmed by massive debt. Two findings against him by bankruptcy court led to the confiscation of the palazzo by the Uffizio

The atrium takes the place of a courtyard. The highly unusual plan of the room consists of two offset squares, and the column supporting the squared arches may be meant to suggest a portico. The capitals and corbels are almost certainly by Benedetto da Rovezzano.

The first two flights of stairs are separated by an ornamental sandstone column, a leitmotif in buildings of the time. Less ordinary are the small elliptical windows, which provide light, and the ceilings of the staircase, with a flat stone panel broken up into a number of bays.

dell'Abbondanza. In order to pay off Borgherini's creditors, the palazzo was sold to the brothers Giovan Antonio, Stefano, and Girolamo di Chiarissimo Rosselli Del Turco, at a price of 7,564 florins. This family still owns the palazzo.

Beginning in the middle of the nineteenth century, the first structural modifications were made. Giovan Battista, son of the marchese Luigi Rosselli Del Turco, had a belvedere built, along with the long terrace high atop the roof. Following the death of Giovan Battista Rosselli Del Turco in 1865, the estate was inherited by his brother, Vincenzo, a canon, and it was he who had a second portal built to the left of the main one. This was done with the division of the interior in mind, so that apartments could be rented separately, as was common practice at that time. When Vincenzo died in 1891, his nephew Antonio once again occupied the entire *piano nobile* himself. It was Antonio who had the main *salone* split up, creating two spectacular little parlors in period style, which were later lavishly furnished.

The palazzo is still split internally, and this has allowed it to be used for numerous purposes. The owners still reside on the top floor, while the second floor houses a renowned Italian fashion group.

The main hall of the second floor is a highly original construction. The joisted beam ceiling was created by woodworkers working under Baccio d'Agnolo (it was restored and rebuilt in the nineteenth century), and is painted teal-blue and gold. Only one of the studded shutters on the windows actually dates from the sixteenth century; the others were built to resemble the one surviving shutter at the end of the nineteenth century, at the wishes of Antonio Rosselli del Turco. Note the united coats-of-arms of the Rosselli and Ricciardi families, and the stained-glass inserts in the windows, with the colored escutcheons of the owners. Every element contributes to an overall sixteenth-century appearance.

Palazzo Ginori

The Ginori family made their fortune in the lucrative trade of banking, and invested more than once in real estate in the quarter of San Lorenzo, where they lived not far from the old basilica of San Lorenzo. At the turn of the sixteenth century, the leading member in this family was Carlo di Lionardo Ginori, who distinguished himself by his competent efforts in more than one public office, and by his marked predilection for patronage of the arts (he liked to surround himself with artists and writers, and among his many protégés was Andrea del Sarto).

Carlo di Lionardo Ginori paid 1,500 florins in 1515 for a house and two small *casette,* which had belonged to the Ubaldini da Pesciola until that family died out. These buildings were also located in the section of Borgo San Lorenzo that was later known as Via Ginori. Beginning in 1516 Carlo di Lionardo Ginori had these buildings demolished, to make way for the fine palazzo that he intended to construct for himself.

Baccio d'Agnolo was one of the many artists who moved in the circle of Carlo di

The facade of Palazzo Ginori was in all likelihood the work of Baccio d'Agnolo. This sharply angled photograph shows the regular progression of the windows, the marked projection of the eaves, and the majestic Ginori family coat-of-arms, in stone. There is another such escutcheon, in polychrome terra-cotta, in the courtyard (detail, top).

The original configuration of the courtyard dates back to the sixteenth century. It has porticoes on all four sides, and is luminous and intimate, with elaborate capitals and corbel brackets. On the walls, part of the remarkable religious frescoes still survive. The original overall appearance, however, has been lost. In the middle of the nineteenth century, the engineer Felice Francolini—at the behest of Lorenzo Ginori Lisci and his wife Ottavia Strozzi— supervised the construction of a new marble-inlaid floor. The courtyard was enclosed with a glass skylight, and an elegant little statuette atop a column was installed.

Lionardo Ginori. We know that Baccio was summoned at one point to arbitrate a dispute concerning boundaries of the property upon which the palazzo was being erected. We further know that Baccio was commissioned by Carlo Ginori to do a number of pieces for the Villa di Torre di Baroncoli, near Calenzano, the Ginoris' home town, from which they had moved to Florence at the end of the thirteenth century. For these reasons, and because of the appearance of a number of elements in the facade and the courtyard, several scholars have identified the palazzo on what is now Via Ginori as a creation of Baccio d'Agnolo.

Plausible though it may be, this hypothesis is not supported by any direct evidence. It is also impossible to ignore the great number of similarities between this palazzo and the one on Via dei Servi, property of the Niccolini family, and attributed with certainty to Domenico d'Agnolo, Baccio's son who was also an architect.

Built between 1516 and 1520, the new home was particularly impressive, towering over the other houses that lined the streets of the quarter. It stood three stories tall, and was crowned by a loggia. There were six vertical bays of windows and an off-center portal in line with the fourth bay, flanked by five little rectangular windows on the ground floor and a distinctive *panca di via* (streetside bench)

The colorful ceiling of a vestibule on the second floor features a nineteenth-century panel with an unusually Christ-like Zeus at the center of an elaborate array of geometric patterns and grotesque decorative motifs. The Zeus, however Christian, is shown with the classical attribute of the eagle, and is dispatching his messenger, Mercury; the other panel features Hera, with her customary attribute, the peacock.

One recurring element in the palazzo is the gilt and white stuccowork. The stuccoes shown (by Carlo Marcellini) surround the great ceiling of the so-called Sala del Fuoco (Hall of the Fire), on which Alessandro Gherardini painted *The Cyclopes* at the turn of the eighteenth century (right). Also note the epigram solemnly framed beneath two putti (top): "What is death to others is true peace to me." The majestic and theatrical stuccoes simulate heavy draperies in a corridor on the second floor (opposite); these too date from the eighteenth century. Amidst the heavy folds of cloth nestle putti, bearing the joint heraldic crests of the Ginori and Rucellai families (in commemoration of a wedding in 1699 linking both clans). In that same corridor there is a small Hermes in a niche, conferring a classical note to the whole area.

that was removed in the nineteenth century. The entire building showed a marked upward thrust in its design, counterbalanced by the sharply projecting eaves.

The courtyard, which was porticoed on four sides, was exquisitely adorned with fine capitals and brackets. When Carlo Ginori died in 1527, the palazzo was inherited by his nephew Lionardo, who married Caterina di Tommaso Soderini, a woman who was renowned for her great love of the arts. She was also notorious as the aunt of Lorenzino de' Medici, the son of Pierfrancesco and Maria Soderini. Lorenzino dangled the bait of an amorous encounter with Caterina to lure Duke Alessandro de' Medici into his palazzo, where he was ambushed and murdered. Since that time, the *casa principale* of the Ginori family has remained the property of the descendents of Lionardo and Caterina, and has undergone a number of substantial changes.

Between 1691 and 1701 the palazzo was enlarged under the supervision of the architect Lorenzo Merlini to take advantage of a small house with garden on Via della Stufa that had been acquired by the Ginori. Merlini built a complex that enclosed the small garden and fountain on three sides, with a balustraded terrace on the second floor.

Inside, the reception halls were lavishly frescoed and decorated by Antonio Ferri, Alessandro Gherardini, and Gian Domenico Ferretti.

The decades that followed saw a further expansion, with the purchase of an adjoining house that had once belonged to Baccio Bandinelli, and a thorough-going renovation of the furnishings in order to live up to the Palazzo's new social reputation. Other work was done under the supervision of the engineer Felice Francolini in the mid-nineteenth century, when the palazzo belonged to the marchese Lorenzo Ginori Lisci, a member of a branch of the Ginori family.

Lorenzo had the palazzo paved in marble, enclosed the courtyard with a cast-iron and glass skylight, and built a broad, handsome stairway, to replace the steep original staircase.

Since then, the palazzo has undergone nothing more serious than changes in the furnishings and decorations, in accordance with the tastes of various eras. And at the end of the nineteenth century, during the lifetime of the many-faceted marchese Carlo Benedetto Ginori, the second-story *salone* was the site of a celebrated and popular five-year series of literary conferences, organized by the marchese himself.

The palazzo still belongs to the Ginori Lisci family, which resides there.

The door of a room on the second floor has elegant gilt decorations and a remarkable, finely chased door handle in the shape of a butterfly.

The garden was added to the rest of the building only at the end of the seventeenth century, when the vegetable garden behind a newly purchased house overlooking Via della Stufa was modified and added to the structure of the building. The architect Lorenzo Merlini created the central facade, the two side facades, the gate that opens onto the street behind the building, and the balcony with railing that runs around the entire area.

Palazzo Niccolini

This angled view shows the great similarity between this facade, built by Domenico di Baccio d'Agnolo, and the facade of Palazzo Ginori. Everything corresponds, from the ground floor to the majestic upper-floor loggia.

Opposite The creation of the rear facade was more complex, and spanned two separate phases. First came the ground-floor loggia, built by Giovanni Antonio Dosio at the behest of Giovanni Niccolini at the end of the sixteenth century. This was followed by the second-story loggia, identical to its ground-floor counterpart, but dating from the mid-seventeenth century. It was built at the wishes of Filippo di Giovanni Niccolini. The resulting structure is quite remarkable in appearance.

Between 1548 and 1550, Bastiano Ciaini da Montauto, a noted and wealthy merchant, engaged the services of Domenico d'Agnolo, a renowned architect and woodworker, and the son of Baccio d'Agnolo. Bastiano asked Domenico to build him a fitting palazzo on the street that then ran straight toward the square on which fronts the sanctuary of the Santissima Annunziata (Our Lady of the Holy Annunciation). And Domenico, clearly wishing to erect a well proportioned, tall building, took clear inspiration—one might say total inspiration—from the palazzo of the Marchesi Ginori, which many consider to have been designed by Baccio d'Agnolo. The resulting facade was nearly identical to that of its model and inspiration, with a streetside bench, and rectangular windows on the ground floor. The courtyard is considerably more original; it is porticoed on four sides, each side partitioned into three arches. The upper two floors are rendered even taller by the elegant architraved windows, surmounted by stringcourse cornices and a series of oculi.

Over time the rear facade proved to be more striking still. It overlooks the garden, and was embellished with two graceful loggias; one corresponding to the ground floor, the other to the second floor.

By the time these loggias were built, however, the palazzo had a new owner. In fact, Bastiano da Montauto had engendered a great many

daughters, but had no son to serve as heir. When Bastiano died, therefore, the entire estate passed over to his nephew, Benedetto, the son of Bastiano's brother Matteo. In order to get out of a financial scrape, Benedetto was forced to sell all his real estate, and the palazzo on Via dei Servi was purchased by Giovanni di Agnolo Niccolini, of an ancient and aristocratic family that had given more than one leading citizen to the Florentine Republic.

Giovanni Niccolini was a senator, and was dedicated to the law, like many in his family. He lived in Rome for many years as an ambassador; at the same time he sponsored the construction of a family chapel in the church of Santa Croce, designed and built by Giovanni Antonio Dosio. Dosio often worked for Niccolini—so often that for a certain period of time he lived in the palazzo itself. It seems quite likely that he designed the ground-floor loggia of the rear facade. Giovanni Niccolini also embellished his Florentine home with fine works of art and Roman antiquities.

Giovanni's son, Filippo Niccolini, oversaw the construction of the second-floor loggia on the rear facade at the turn of the seventeenth century; moreover he was responsible for commissioning, over the course of three decades, most of the frescoes that decorate the halls. This project was carried forward by a series of noted artists: the Volterrano, Giacinto Gemignani, Angelo Michele Colonna (who

Domenico di Baccio d'Agnolo also built the well lighted courtyard, with triple arcades topped with keystones; on the floor above, overlooking the courtyard, are architraved windows with distinctive cornicework and oculi.

Opposite The windows and oculi are equally striking viewed from this corridor overlooking the courtyard. The wooden finishings, massive ceiling, and austere furnishings are all typical of the sixteenth-century.

Following pages Two of the most impressive rooms on the second floor are unquestionably the Studio del Provveditore (page 258), with its handsome coffered ceiling with gilt decorations; and the anteroom (page 259), embellished with an elegant frieze and another coffered ceiling with rosettes. In the first of the two rooms there is a sixteenth-century fireplace, which is believed to have been built by Domenico di Baccio d'Agnolo. The mantelpiece is adorned with lion's heads (heraldic attribute of the Niccolini family) and trophies.

created the entire decorative array of the gallery), Jacopo Chiavistelli, and Antonio Ciseri. Because Filippo died in 1666 without male offspring, his palazzo became the inheritance of the senator Lorenzo Niccolini, from a collateral branch of the Niccolini di Camugliano. This branch of the family, in turn, was forced to sell the palazzo through a remarkable bureaucratic imbroglio having to do with the inheritance laws; this, after they had paid for futher painting of rooms during the course of the eighteenth century. They sold it in 1824 to Count Dmitri Bouturline, counsellor of the Czar, and an impassioned bibliophile.

While part of the quarters in the palazzo were rented out, others were prepared to accommodate the collection of venerable old books belonging to the new owner. During this period, the garden was rearranged, and the facade overlooking Via dei Servi was decorated in *graffiti* and frescoes. This was done by a number of artists, including Bandinelli, Valtancoli, Sarti, and Zucconi. In 1918— the year after the Russian Revolution—the Bouturline family sold the palazzo to the Pinucci family. Eleven years later, that family sold it to the Federazione dei Fasci di Combattimento di Firenze, a Fascist veteran's organization; the palazzo served as headquarters for the organization for many years. With the fall of Fascism, the building became the property of the Ministero dei Lavori Pubblici (Italian

Most of the frescoes that adorn the halls, the second-floor gallery, and the ground-floor rooms date from the seventeenth century. Among those on the ground floor, the work of the Volterrano stands out in particular (note his depiction, left, middle, of *Beauty Mistreated by Time*, set in an elaborate gilt frame), as does the work of Giacinto Gemignani, who painted *Mount Parnassus* (detail, opposite) in remarkably vivid colors. There are a great many frescoes with mythological subjects.

Ministry for Public Works), which still owns it. At the end of the 1950s, the ministry undertook a massive restoration and reorganization of the palazzo to recover its original architectural lines and splendid painted decorations.

Palazzo Pucci

The earliest, original part of the facade is certainly the central area, with a large portal surmounted by a majestic Serlian window and a little balcony.

The large palazzo that occupies much of Via dei Pucci—and which, in terms of size, length, and number of windows, seems to be one of the most impressive buildings in Florence—has only acquired these features in the relatively recent past. For many years it was nothing more than a *casa,* and not a palazzo at all.

The Pucci came to Florence from the country in the thirteenth century, and quickly acquired a prestigious reputation that was clearly endorsed by the numerous public offices that family members were summoned to fill. One of the factors that clearly encouraged their rise in favor was their steady adherence to the Medici family. Puccio Pucci was one of the most determined leaders of the pro-Medici faction during the lifetime of Cosimo the Elder; when Cosimo was exiled from Florence, Puccio openly worked to bring him quickly back. When the situation changed in Cosimo's favor, he rewarded Puccio generously. At this time (in the early fifteenth century), the Pucci family was already split into two main branches, one headed by Puccio, the other by his brother Saracino.

Puccio Pucci possessed a number of houses in the area now occupied by Via dei Servi, not far from the Ospedale di Santa Maria Nuova. His descendants continued to live in those houses, and carried on his pro-Medici policies, at times taking them to extremes. Giannozzo, a

The present-day size of the palazzo is such that more than one courtyard can easily coexist here, though there is customarily only one courtyard per palazzo. The courtyards date from the early years, and clearly once belonged to two separate residential buildings. Note in particular the broad portico (top)—like a hallway in its configuration—that leads into the central courtyard (opposite). The unusual feature of this courtyard is that it is surrounded by solid walls.

nephew of Puccio, was in fact beheaded for plotting to bring Pietro II the Unfortunate back to Florence during the second exile of the Medici.

Around 1450, Puccio's son Antonio purchased the group of houses, including *piazza* and vegetable garden, that can fairly be considered the core of the future palazzo.

Meanwhile, the family's power was waxing constantly: the Pucci family had established ties with Pope Paul III Farnese, and by the turn of the sixteenth century, boasted a number of senators and no fewer than three cardinals.

One of those cardinals, Roberto Pucci, was the fifth son of Antonio di Puccio. Before setting out in his ecclesiastical career, Roberto had been married to a daughter of the historian Francesco Guicciardini. She had borne him a son named Pandolfo. This son "distinguished" himself by coming up with a plot against the grand duke Cosimo I (the first Pucci to turn against the Medici!) and was hanged.

His son, Orazio, was determined to avenge his father's death, and he too wound up on the gallows, under Francesco I.

This rash behavior led to the confiscation of all the Pucci family's possessions, a harsh judgement that was overruled by the grand duke himself, who was aware of the merit the family had shown over the years.

In the very years in which these decisions were being made, the Pucci family began

Many rooms on the second floor are decorated with fine frescoes from the seventeenth and nineteenth centuries, by Giovanni da San Giovanni, Gian Domenico Ferretti, Giuseppe Bezzuoli, and Luigi Ademollo. The ceiling of a room on the second floor (opposite), is decorated with false architecture in a clear pursuit of perspective.

to enlarge their chief home. This home, upon the death of Lorenzo di Antonio in 1531, had become the property of his brother, Roberto, and was subsequently inherited by Roberto's children, who spent immense sums to decorate and improve it.

This building must have corresponded roughly to the central section of the present-day palazzo, which indeed stands out for its particularly exquisite architectural composition and its decorations. In addition, there were the houses on either side, which remained distinct and separate.

When the Puccio branch of the family died out in 1612, the entire estate was inherited by the heirs of Saracino, specifically the senator Niccolò Pucci. Thanks to the separate buildings, when Niccolò died, his sons were able to break up the inheritance with relative ease: Giulio received the central palazzo, while Alessandro received the houses on the corner of Via dei Servi.

Giulio's son, Orazio Pucci, purchased a number of houses that stood on the other side of his property, and in 1688 he asked Paolo Falconieri to unify all of the facades to go with the facade of the central structure. And because Giulio's heirs did much the same thing at the turn of the eighteenth century, it finally became possible to speak of a true Palazzo Pucci.

The palazzo, however, has remained split into two parts. There is the larger half, which includes the nucleus of the

The long gallery filled with refined furnishings, exquisite paintings, and numerous objets-d'art is a vast setting for receiving guests.

entire complex, once the
property of the Pucci di
Barsento branch of the family.
This half still has the two
courtyards of the two core
residential structures that it
originally comprised. The
halls in this half were richly
frescoed in the eighteenth
century by Giuseppe Bezzuoli
and Luigi Ademollo. The
ballroom was decorated with
stuccoes, which were redone
at the behest of the senator
Orazio Roberto Pucci at the
end of the eighteenth century. Lastly, the recent addition of a "roadway" runs
through entranceways and
courtyards, and provides a
handy way into the ground-
floor rooms.

This part of the palazzo was
split up in this century
between the two sons of the
Marchese Emilio Pucci. It is
safe to say that, despite a renovation here and there, the
building boasts an excellent
state of preservation.

The other portion of the
large building, which overlooks Via dei Servi, has both
its own entrance and its own
courtyard, as well as a set of
notable frescoes by Giovanni
da San Giovanni occupying a
few of the halls. After a series
of owners, the palazzo wound
up in the hands of the Mensa
Arcivescovile di Firenze (Dining Hall of the Archbishops,
Florence). It is still owned by
the local Curia of the Roman
Catholic Church.

Among the more notable
facts concerning this palazzo
is that the well known Circolo Artistico, one of the
leading artistic organizations

The great ballroom is marked by
the pale, subtle shades of the
walls and ceiling. Renovated at
the end of the eighteenth century,
it features classical busts set
above the cornices that top the
doorways.

in this city, had its headquarters here between 1887 and 1888. All of the leading painters of the Macchiaioli school frequented this building. Indeed, the inauguration of the Circolo Artistico in Palazzo Pucci was presided over by no less a personage than Margherita of Savoy,

This fresco occupies the entire wall of a large room. The pastoral scene is classically eighteenth-century, with the idylls of the bath, the background that merges into the countryside, and the presence among the female figures of a dark-skinned lady-in-waiting.

queen of Italy.

Finally, there is an odd bit of history surrounding a window that has been bricked up at the corner of Via dei Servi. It is said that one of the conspiring henchmen of Pandolfo Pucci crept out this window on his way to attempt to assassinate Cosimo I.

Palazzo Corsini in Parione

There is a palazzo in Florence that has its main entrance on Via del Parione, yet it overlooks the banks of the river Arno with an impressively long balcony and a thoroughly distinctive appearance. Indeed, the river-front facade has very few of the features normally found in the more classical homes of the Florentine aristocracy. This is the palazzo of the Corsini family. In terms of the time of its construction and its overall appearance, this palazzo fits into none of the Florentine architectural categories examined thus far. In fact, it is far more similar in typology to the palazzo found in Rome. It has many links to the Palazzo di Gino Capponi, which is treated later in this book.

On this site in the sixteenth century stood the houses of Bindo Altoviti, a wealthy banker and celebrated patron of the arts who lived in Rome for many years. He opposed the designs of the Medici with such persistence that he was declared a rebellious outlaw by Cosimo I. His property was seized and his houses were assigned to Don Giovanni, a natural son of the grand duke.

Don Giovanni added new purchases to his estate, had

The facade overlooking the Lungarno, with the portal and the balustraded terrace defining the interior courtyard (which is enclosed by high walls only on three sides), was almost certainly built to plans by Antonio Ferri at the end of the seventeenth century. This palazzo is unusual by Florentine standards, and in a sense it was left unfinished, because the plans called for it to be extended further to the left and encompass the existing houses to acquire a perfect symmetry. The building does include the familiar escutcheon and other carved stone decorations.

the houses decorated, and surrounded them with gardens, creating a sort of country lodge, in the midst of the city. Here he loved to gather his friends and hold sumptuous banquets. After his death in 1621, the property passed to Don Lorenzo de' Medici, the son of Ferdinand I, who showed the same predilection for hosting banquets. Particularly notorious was the huge banquet he hosted in 1630 in honor of the members of the Accademia della Crusca, a learned society. A detailed and astonished description of it survives in the letters of Francesco Redi.

When Don Lorenzo died, the Medici decided to sell off the entire complex; in 1640, it was purchased for the sum of 14,150 *scudi*, coins of the grand duchy, by Maddalena Machiavelli, widow of a Corsini, who immediately deeded it to her eighteen-year-old son, the marchese Bartolommeo Corsini. It was he who set about the radical project of renovation that was soon to transform the appearance of the palazzo.

In 1650, the architect Alfonso Parigi the Younger was assigned to undertake the restoration of the original *casino*. Then Bartolommeo Corsini asked Ferdinando Tacca—son of the better-known Pietro Tacca—to enlarge the building. He built the impressive facade overlooking Via del Parione, with twenty-three vertical bays of windows. This facade may have been based on designs by Alfonso Parigi.

Work continued at a good

This impressive stairway (opposite) was built between 1694 and 1695 at the behest of Filippo Corsini by architect Antonio Ferri. Majestic in appearance, dominated by the joint escutcheons of the Corsini and Rinuccini families (Filippo's wife was a Rinuccini), the staircase now features a large statue of Pope Clement XII, who was Lorenzo Corsini before his elevation, giving a benediction (left). Carved in Rome and sent to Florence by the pontiff himself, the statue was placed here in 1737 by Ticciati, after the idea of placing it in the main hall of the *piano nobile* was abandoned.

clip until 1671, when a series of interruptions ensued. Despite them, an elegant spiral staircase was built by Pier Francesco Silvani. When the marchese Bartolommeo Corsini died in 1685, his son and heir, Filippo, cracked the whip. Work began again in earnest: in 1686 he obtained permission to build a long balcony overlooking the banks of the Arno. It was designed and built by the architect Antonio Ferri, as were the elevations overlooking the courtyard. Following this, work went forward, respectively, on the new second-floor *salone* (main hall); on the monumental staircase (1694–95); and, lastly, on the remarkable grotto on the ground floor. During this same period (1695–1700) the rooms and halls in the wing of the palazzo extending toward Ponte a Santa Trinita were frescoed. Antonio Domenico Gabbiani did the *salone* and the gallery overlooking the Arno; Piero Dandini did the rooms overlooking Via del Parione; and Tommaso Gherardini did the bedroom, with the halls of Ceres and the Arts. Under Filippo's son, named Bartolommeo like his grandfather, all work was finally completed. The young Bartolommeo oversaw the completion of the wing of the palazzo extending toward Ponte alla Carraia. Once that wing was complete, the facade overlooking the Arno gained the distinctive baroque appearance—in many ways exquisitely Roman—that

The ballroom (opposite) is among the halls that were built and decorated at the end of the seventeenth century. The large, distinctive ceiling is surrounded by white-and-gilt stuccoes, with fine modeling. On a light-blue background, the mythological figures so dear to the artists of the period appear in throngs: nymphs are surrounded by putti, crowned with garlands; nereids and tritons emerge from the sea.

Opposite The gallery with large windows overlooking the courtyard probably dates back to the seventeenth century. Entirely frescoed with trompe-l'oeil elements, the gallery is attributed to Antonio Domenico Gabbiani; note the fine ceiling studded with ornaments of faux architecture, which also appear in the lunettes.
At the center is an oval in which the Chariot of the Sun is depicted (bottom); the heraldic crest of the Corsini family adorns the rear of the chariot.

aroused such perplexity among the Florentines. The central structure, on a line with the courtyard, was sharply recessed, and the two wings were surmounted by statues—none of which was in tune with the architecture of the city or prevailing tastes. Still, the whole structure was soon accepted as a remarkably striking piece of architecture.

The palazzo, then, was definitively completed in 1735. In the same general period, a Corsini had been made pope, as Clement XII; this was Lorenzo Corsini, the brother of the same Filippo who had done so much to build this new palazzo.

As if to pronounce good the splendid new palazzo, the pope sent a statue of himself to Florence, and Girolamo Ticciati—after considering a number of alternatives, including that of placing it in full view in the enormous ball room—decided to place it on the first landing of the monumental staircase. This was done in 1737.

From that time on, the palazzo was the site of continual entertaining and receiving, especially during the time of the prince, Lorenzo, who was the Grand Prior of Pisa of the Order of Malta, thanks to the benevolent interest of his great-uncle the pope. Lorenzo gave memorable feasts and parties; he loved to surround himself with artists, and filled his court with them. When French troops arrived in Florence at the end of the eighteenth century, the

elderly prince chose to take refuge in Vienna. His palazzo thus came to be the new home of General Murat and his family; later it became the meeting place of the most determined supporters of Elisa Baciocchi, Napoleon Bonaparte's sister. When the grand duke returned to the city, the palazzo enjoyed a new moment of splendor in 1870 when, at the order of the new king, Victor Emmanuel II of Savoy, its halls were used for the official reception of the delegation that had come from Madrid to offer the Spanish crown to Prince Amadeus of Aosta. Moreover, at the behest of the Prince Tommaso, until the early years of the twentieth century, the palazzo continued to host a great annual ball, to which all the chief authorities of the city were invited.

The palazzo still belongs to the Corsini family. During the twentieth century the family has been faced with two catastrophic events. In 1944 German explosives damaged the structure of the palazzo, and in 1966 the terrible flood of the river Arno devastated the ground floor and the basement, including the remarkable grotto. The damage was soon repaired, and in time the building was restored to its former splendor. Visitors can still admire the halls of the gallery, containing the leading private art collection in Florence, and in a well-ventilated attic, one of Florence's leading painters, Luciano Guarnieri, has established his studio.

The vast *salone* on the second floor is one of the largest in Florence. It too was planned and built by Ferri around 1690, and presents a number of interesting features, including the balcony that runs around the entire hall, richly decorated with statues and busts. The ceiling is by Antonio Domenico Gabbiani, and dates from 1695–1700. At the center of the fresco (left), which depicts an *Apotheosis of the Corsini Family*, is a model of the palazzo as seen from the Lungarno, borne prominently aloft.

Palazzo Portinari Salviati

Along the Corso, one of the main streets of early Florence, the names and histories of two families were bound up with one another, and became famous.

Along this street, as early as the thirteenth century, the Portinari family owned a number of houses. The Portinari were well-to-do bankers, and over the course of the fifteenth century, many of the Portinari were partners in or served as officers of the Banco Mediceo di Milano or the Banco Mediceo di Bruges. (One of them, Folco Portinari, was traditionally said to have been the father of Dante's Beatrice.) Moreover, they had close ties with the great architect Michelozzo. It is not unreasonable to think that they asked Michelozzo to design the great palazzo that was to replace their several houses in the Corso.

Tommaso Portinari, in particular, was known throughout the business world of Europe. It seems that he may have paid for the first phase of construction in the area surrounding the courtyard; he may also have been behind the construction of a unified facade, when the composite building first attained a clear physiognomy.

The facade on the Corso as it appears today is the result of a series of enlargements. The original two-story facade had only seven vertical bays of windows; it was enlarged for the first time around 1570. At the end of the seventeenth century it was further elongated, with the incorporation of the houses and workshops that stood to its left. It finally extended to the corner of Via dello Studio. The massive portal with rusticated cornicework is therefore in an asymmetrical location with respect to the rest of the facade. In appearance, this portal greatly resembles the coat-of-arms of the Portinari family, which is reproduced here in two different versions. The first is in stone, while the second is stitched in fabric, and appears in the altar frontal of the chapel.

This splendid courtyard is a true architectural gem. Because of the twelve bronze heads that appear in the niches, it has been named the Courtyard of the Emperors. Its clear and linear architectural structure qualifies it as a masterpiece of early Mannerism; note the columns, oculi, and curved and broken pediments. The vaults were decorated from 1574 on by Alessandro Allori and his assistants Giovanni Maria Butteri, Giovanni Fiammingo, Alessandro di Benedetto, and Giovanni Bizzelli.

Over the course of the sixteenth century, the fortunes of the Portinari family declined steadily. They were forced to sell off the houses along the Corso, one by one, to another family whose fortunes were steadily improving: the Salviati.

The Salviati family had been particularly prominent in the time of the Florentine Republic, and had produced many leading citizens, sixty-three Priori (heads of guilds), and twenty-one Gonfalonieri (rulers of Florence). The family reputation gained great luster when Iacopo di Giovanni Salviati married one of the daughters of Lorenzo the Magnificent—Lucrezia de' Medici—followed by the otherwise unhappy marriage between Maria Salviati and Giovanni dalle Bande Nere, which did however produce Cosimo, the future first grand duke of Tuscany.

As early as the beginning of the sixteenth century, the Salviati began to purchase the houses along the Corso that belonged to the Portinari, and in 1546 they received the deed to the new palazzo. The first family member to own it was Iacopo di Alamanno, first cousin of Cosimo, the new grand duke. Nearly thirty years after purchasing it, spanning the years between 1572 and 1578, Iacopo carried out a great series of decorative improvements. He had a garden installed behind the palazzo, and enclosed the garden with a loggia; he built a little chapel, and a lovely courtyard. The courtyard was

The series of decorations in the Courtyard of the Emperors flows into the adjoining room. In that room, on a ceiling decorated with grotesques and landscapes, appear the *Stories of Hercules*, while in the courtyard, set in panels with an analogous decorative pattern, are stories taken from the *Odyssey*.

later known as the Cortile degli Imperatori (Courtyard of the Emperors); it was completely frescoed by Alessandro Allori (with assistants). Allori also painted a number of canvases that were hung in the many halls of the palazzo. He was a renowned architect, and had been appointed to replace Bartolomeo Ammannati as the director of construction of the Opera del Duomo (as the cathedral, Santa Maria del Fiore, was officially called while under construction). It is likely that Allori built other sections of the palazzo, but no documents have survived to prove this. There are even scholars who claim that Ammannati worked on Palazzo Portinari at some point, though again this is without evidence. We do know that the twelve busts of Roman emperors distributed throughout the courtyard in niches were purchased in Venice in 1575.

At the end of the seventeenth century, the palazzo and the facade on the left side were enlarged in order to make room for the increasingly demanding social life of the inhabitants (the spectacular entertaining that was done here lived on in Florentine memory); carriages were thus afforded easier entrance as well.

The eighteenth century began with a memorable gala held to honor twenty-seven members of the Accademia della Crusca, a learned society, on the evening of September 18, 1701. The evening culminated in an elaborate

On the *piano nobile* is the meeting room of the board of directors of the Banca Toscana (below, left); the room has a late-eighteenth-century frescoed ceiling by Tommaso Gherardini and assistants. It depicts Mettus Curtius leaping into the chasm on horseback (detail, left), and is a masterpiece of cunning perspective. On the wall is *The Study*, a painting by Felice Carena.

Opposite The large fresco that adorns the ceiling of this gallery dates from the eighteenth century, and is attributed to Tommaso Gherardini. It was painted at the wishes of Niccolò Maria Ricciardi Serguidi. The fresco depicts *Mt. Olympus*, flanked by allegories of *Day and Night*. It was done with a clearly anti-baroque technique and narrative approach. In this same room hang some of the artworks from the vast collection of the Banca Toscana.

The ceiling of the Studio del Direttore, or office of the president, was frescoed by Tommaso Gherardini and assistants, and depicts *The Four Seasons*.

banquet, held in the loggia surrounding the courtyard.

If the century began gloriously, it continued with the extinction of the main branch of the Salviati family in 1704. As a result the palazzo passed into the hands of a branch of the family, that descended from Antonio, son of the senator Filippo.

The new owners were in time to offer fitting hospitality to the king of Denmark, Frederick Augustus IV, in 1708, under legendary circumstances. When the Danish sovereign was a young prince and the heir apparent, he had traveled to Italy, and visited Lucca. There he met a young noblewoman of the Dei Trenta family. Love blossomed between them, but for dynastic reasons, that love could not be sanctioned by marriage. The heir apparent returned to Denmark, abandoning the young girl. She, in despair, decided to become a nun. Once he became king, Frederick Augustus returned to Florence, expressly to see the woman he had loved years before. Because she was in a cloistered convent, it was quite difficult to obtain permission to see her, but in the end he won out. They met in the Florentine convent of Santa Maria Maddalena dei Pazzi. The two former lovers spoke at length in the presence of another nun. All that is known of their conversation is that the young woman tried more than once to persuade Frederick Augustus to convert to Roman Catholicism.

The shift in ownership at

The large Salone della Presidenza (hall of the chairman) on the second floor has an original wooden lacunar ceiling dating from the fifteenth century. It is decorated with friezes with the usual attributes of the Portinari family, the lion and the door. Hanging on the wall is *The Purification of the Virgin Mary*, by Francesco Morandini, known as the Poppi.

the turn of the eighteenth century marked a new direction in the fate of the palazzo. As the decades passed, the steady application of matrimonial politics loosened the bonds between the Salviati and the city of Florence, and strengthened their ties to Rome. In 1768, following the marriage of the last descendant of the family, Anna Maria Luisa Salviati, to Prince Marc'Antonio Borghese, the palazzo was sold to Niccolò Serguidi. It was Serguidi who paid for the decoration of the halls on the second floor and the gallery. We know that the palazzo belonged to the Da Cepperello family in 1816, that it became property of the state in 1865, and that it was used as the main office of the Ministry of Justice. In 1870 it became property of the city of Florence, and later the Cassa di Risparmio di Firenze. In 1881 it became property of the Padri Scolopi, a religious order, and for many years they ran their religious schools in the palazzo. Finally, in 1921, the bank Credito Toscano purchased the original home of the Portinari to make it into the main office of the Banca Toscana, which it remains. The Banca Toscana financed extensive restoration, rehung the paintings by Alessandro Allori, and restored an enormous apartment on the second floor for entertaining and receptions. A number of rooms now display the art collection that the bank has assembled over the years.

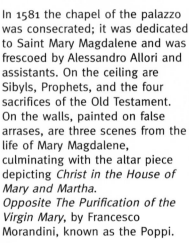

In 1581 the chapel of the palazzo was consecrated; it was dedicated to Saint Mary Magdalene and was frescoed by Alessandro Allori and assistants. On the ceiling are Sibyls, Prophets, and the four sacrifices of the Old Testament. On the walls, painted on false arrases, are three scenes from the life of Mary Magdalene, culminating with the altar piece depicting *Christ in the House of Mary and Martha*.
Opposite The Purification of the Virgin Mary, by Francesco Morandini, known as the Poppi.

Palazzo di Gino Capponi

The majestic facade of Palazzo Capponi was built at the turn of the eighteenth century according to plans by Carlo Fontana on behalf of the senator Alessandro Capponi. Its immense size, its vast number of windows, the large portal surmounted by a small balcony and the escutcheon of the family that built it—all of these features take this palazzo out of the realm of the usual Florentine standards, and place it into the class of the royal palace.

The palazzi of Florence—with all their typological and chronological variations—tend to present a relatively repetitive, conventional appearance. It is thus fairly easy to identify the typical Florentine palazzo.

There is one building, however, of comparatively recent vintage (dating from the eighteenth century), set close to the great ring roads, and only a short distance away from the Palazzo Della Gherardesca—that does not quite fit in. This building was clearly inspired, in size, splendor, and design, by the Roman palazzi of the time. The building is known as the Palazzo di Gino Capponi, although the man who actually ordered it built was the senator Alessandro Capponi. Capponi was a member of an illustrious and aristocratic Florentine family, with venerable historical roots; among its forefathers was the renowned Florentine patriot Pier Capponi, who courageously led the defense of the city against the troops of Charles VIII, King of France, who invaded Italy in 1495–96.

The Capponi were one of the oldest and noblest families in Florence (and, as we have seen, they already owned the so-called Palazzo Capponi delle Rovinate on Via de' Bardi). In the eighteenth century, moreover, they were also quite wealthy, thanks to their profitable activities in business and trade. Senator Alessandro Capponi, who lived between the late-seventeenth and

The facade that overlooks the garden, which is also by Fontana, appears livelier than the streetside facade. Here, two side wings project forward, and there is a large portico on the ground floor. Various lines of balconies extend up to the balustrade atop the third floor.

The garden is vast and entrancing.
It was completed in the
eighteenth century, and is dotted
with flowerbeds, trees, and
shrubs, all set around a central
fountain. On one side, the garden
is enclosed by a remarkable aviary
(opposite).

Palazzo di Gino Capponi

early-eighteenth centuries, was one of the leading figures in Roman high society. When he returned to Florence in 1699 and married the noble-woman Bianca Ricasoli, it seems he felt a need to build a fragment of the Eternal City in the city of his forefathers. He purchased—from Duke Anton Maria Salviati, a direct descendant of Lorenzo the Magnificent by the female line—the huge estate that had thus far been handed down from father to son in the Medici family. Set just beyond the church of the Santissima Annunziata, the estate possessed a lovely little country lodge, and featured renowned plantations of rare and exotic plants. It was valued at about 12,000 *scudi*, a coin of the time.

The new owner immediately ordered that his new property be surveyed, and that accurate maps be drawn up. In spring of 1702 he ordered these maps sent to Rome, to the architect Carlo Fontana, and asked Fontana to make plans for the construction of an impressive new palazzo.

In August of the same year, in exchange for the sizable fee of 85 *scudi*, Fontana sent plans and a drawing of the new palazzo. An engineer named Alessandro Cecchini immediately set about building it. Construction began with the foundations and the walls of the central structure. As early as the beginning of 1704, it could be said that the central wing was complete up to the fourth floor.

The aviary was begun in 1706 and completed two years later. It is encrusted with sea shells and sponges, surmounted by statues, and crowded with classical decorations. Nowadays it has been converted into a comfortable apartment.

The *salone*, or great hall of the *piano nobile*, however, was not finished quite so speedily; the ceiling was not completed until the end of 1706. This was to be the largest *salone* in all of Florence.

Likewise, the immense staircase was not really finished until 1708; with it, the distinctive aviary was completed. This remarkable structure, decorated with a seashell motif, stood on the left side of the garden.

Overlooking the vast garden is the secondary facade, with the two side wings set forward with respect to the central wing. This facade is actually more distinctive and noteworthy than the main facade. Indeed, the main facade is fairly monotonous, with its nineteen vertical bays of windows; it was completed in a second phase, with a small balcony, the Capponi coat-of-arms, and a stone cornice surrounding the main portal.

By 1710 work on the palazzo was complete; between 1703 and 1704 artists including Atanasio Bimbacci, Cinqui, and Camillo Sagrestani had frescoed most of the rooms.

Alessandro Capponi died in 1716, leaving his estate to his two sons, Scipione and Francesco Maria. They lived in the palazzo, and entertained in it lavishly and often. They spent heavily to furnish it in a fitting manner.

The Capponi palace, with its monumental staircase lined with statues and fountains, its galleries of paintings, and its

The first distinctive feature of the palazzo is, without a doubt, the well lighted staircase (opposite), adorned with statues, fountains, frescoes, and stuccoes. The second is the *salone* (above), certainly the largest one in Florence, with its solid balustrade, the heraldic crests of the Capponi family and other families bound to them through marriage, and paintings by Matteo Bonechi commemorating major episodes in the family's history.

impressive series of frescoes,
soon became an attraction,
drawing illustrious visitors
from all over Europe. At the
end of the eighteenth century, with the death of
Marchese Alessandro Maria
Capponi, the main branch of
the family dwindled to a
close. The palazzo was passed

over to a secondary branch of
the family; the marchese Pier
Roberto Capponi left the
palazzo to his son Gino, who
became a leading personality
in nineteenth-century Florence. A man of great learning and intellect, Gino
Capponi served as president
of the Accademia Colom-
baria. He wrote, with Pietro
Vieusseux, his celebrated

The dining room and the
bedroom, which are now part of
the residence of Dottor Giuseppe
Salvi, are elegantly furnished and
preserved with great care. The
large eighteenth-century frescoes
are still in excellent condition. In
the fresco in the dining room,
among the many figures, we can
make out that of Dante Alighieri.

Antologia. Gino Capponi traveled extensively throughout Europe; he was friends with such major cultural figures as the poet Ugo Foscolo and the writer and statesman Chateaubriand. He transformed his Florentine palazzo into a gathering spot for leading figures in European culture. His home was graced by the presence of the great writers Alessandro Manzoni and Giacomo Leopardi, the poet and satirist Giuseppe Giusti, the poet, historian, and statesman Alfonse de Lamartine, and the politicians and writers Massimo D'Azeglio and Pietro Colletta.

When the marchese Gino Capponi died in 1876, the palazzo and its grounds were inherited by his eldest daughter Marianna, and her husband, the Genoan marchese Gentile Farinola; his family owned the palazzo until 1920.

During these years, the new owners renovated the halls of the huge residence, transforming them into independent suites of apartments. These were rented out to various families, including the Balduino family of Genoa, who were renowned for their princely entertaining.

The palazzo was then purchased by Egisto Fabbri, a wealthy Italian-American businessman, who installed his art collection there. The building was then sold to Italian Senator Alessandro Contini Bonacossi, who hung his own collection of paintings. The Palazzo still belongs to the heirs of Contini Bonacossi.

Also part of the same suite are two drawing rooms (above) and an entrance vestibule (opposite), which is entirely frescoed with trompe-l'oeil architecture. The paintings, which are quite lavish and often enriched with stuccoes, were done between 1703 and 1713, and are one of the most remarkable features of the entire palazzo. Renowned artists of the period worked here, including Atanasio Bimbacci, the Cinqui, Camillo Sagrestani, and Niccolò Lapi.

Selected Bibliography

Bargellini, Piero. *La splendida storia di Firenze*. Florence, 1964.

Berti, Luciano. *Il principe dello Studiolo*. Florence, 1967.

Borsi, Franco. *Firenze nel Cinquecento*. Rome, 1974.

Bucci, Mario and Raffaello Bencini. *Palazzi di Firenze*. Florence, 1971.

Cazzato, Vincenzo and Massimo De Vico Fallani. *Guida ai giardini urbani di Firenze*. Florence, 1981.

Chastel, André. *Art et Humanisme à Florence au temps de Laurent le Magnifique*. Paris, 1959.

Ginori Lisci, Leonardo. *I palazzi di Firenze nella storia e nell'arte*. Florence, 1981.

Goldthwaite, Richard A. "The Florentine Palace and Domestic Architecture," *American Historical Review*, LXXVII, 1972.

——. *The Building of Renaissance Florence*. London, 1980.

Linburger, Walther. *Die Gebäude von Florenz, Architekten, Strassen und Plätze in alphabetischen Verzeichnissen*. Leipzig, 1910.

Marchini, Giuseppe. *Giuliano da Sangallo*. Florence, 1943.

——. "Le finestre 'inginocchiate'," *Antichità Viva*, I, 1976.

——. "Facciate fiorentine," *Antichità Viva*, III, 1978.

Rodolico, Francesco. *Le pietre delle città d'Italia*. Florence, 1953 (second edition, 1964, third edition, 1995).

Ross, Janet. *Florentine Palaces and Their Stories*. London, 1905.

Sanpaolesi, Piero. *Brunelleschi*. Milan, 1962.

——. "La casa fiorentina di Bartolommeo Scala," *Studium zur toskanischen Kunst: Festschrift für L.H. Heydenreich*. Munich, 1964.

Stegmann, Carl von and Heinrich von Geymüller. *Die Architektur der Renaissance in Toskana*. Munich, 1890–1906.

Thiem, Günther and Christel Thiem. *Toskanische Fassadendekoration in Sgraffito und Fresko*. Munich, 1964.

Trotta, Giampaolo. *Gli antichi chiassi tra Ponte Vecchio e Santa Trinita*. Florence, 1992.

Zocchi, Giuseppe. *Scelta di XXIV vedute delle principali contrade, piazze e palazzi della città di Firenze*. Florence, 1744.

Addresses of the palazzi

Casino Torrigiani del Campuccio
Via de' Serragli, 144
Property of the Marchesi
Torrigiani; closed to the public.
Page 180.

Palazzo Antinori
Piazzetta Antinori, 3
Property of the Marchesi Antinori;
the inner courtyard and the garden
are open to the public
Page 116.

Palazzo Bargellini
Via delle Pinzochere, 3
Property of the Bargellini estate;
closed to the public.
Page 200.

Palazzo Bartolini Salimbeni
Piazza Santa Trinita, 1
Property of the Bartolini Salimbeni
estate; the inner courtyard is open
to the public.
Page 194.

Palazzo Budini Gattai
Piazza della Santissima
Annunziata, 1
Property of the Budini Gattai
family; closed to the public.
Page 214.

Palazzo Capponi delle Rovinate
Via de' Bardi, 36
Property of the Counts Capponi;
closed to the public.
Page 170.

Palazzo Cocchi
Piazza S. Croce, 1
Property of the city of Florence;
partly open to the public.
Page 164.

Palazzo Corsini in Parione
Via del Parione, 11/12
Property of the Princes Corsini;
open to the public by
appointment. Call the
Amministrazione Corsini at (55)
210.564.
Page 272.

Palazzo Corsini Suarez
Via Maggio, 42
Property of the city of Florence,
and the site of the Laboratorio di
Restauro (Studio for the
Restoration of Books) and the
Archivio Contemporaneo del
Gabinetto Vieusseux; the archive is
open to the public.
Page 224.

Palazzo Davanzati
Via Porta Rossa
Commission for Environmental
and Architectural Heritage
(Soprintendenza ai Beni
Ambientali e Architettonici);
museum open to the public every
morning except Monday.
Page 96.

Palazzo Della Gherardesca
Borgo Pinti, 99
Property of the Società
Metallurgica Italiana (SMI), an
industrial corporation; closed to
the public.
Page 140.

Palazzo Feroni
Via Tornabuoni, 2
Property of the Ferragamo family;
partly open to the public.
Page 80.

Palazzo di Gino Capponi
Via G. Capponi, 26
Various owners; closed to the
public.
Page 294.

Palazzo Ginori
Via dei Ginori, 11
Property of the Marchese Lorenzo
Ginori; closed to the public.
Page 246.

Palazzo Giugni
Via degli Alfani, 48
Property of the engineer
Fraschetti; closed to the public.
Page 206.

Palazzo Gondi
Piazza San Firenze, 2
Property of the Marchesi Gondi;
the inner courtyard is open to the
public.
Page 148.

Palazzo Malenchini Alberti
Via dei Benci, 1
Property of the Marchesi
Malenchini; closed to the public.
Page 88.

Palazzo Medici Riccardi
Via Cavour, 1
Offices of the Province of Florence
and the Prefecture; open to the
public.
Page 50.

Palazzo Niccolini
Via dei Servi, 15
Site of the Tuscan office of public
works (Provveditorato alle Opere
Pubbliche della Regione Toscana);
closed to the public.
Page 254.

Palazzo Nonfinito
Via del Proconsolo, 12
Site of the Istituto di Antropologia
e Etnologia of the Università di
Firenze, a university institute of
anthropology and ethnology; the
inner courtyard and the museum
are open to the public.
Page 188.

Palazzo Pitti
Piazza Pitti
Commission for Environmental
and Architectural Heritage
(Soprintendenza ai Beni
Ambientali e Architettonici); open
to the public.
Page 66.

Palazzo Portinari Salviati
Via del Corso, 6
Property of the Banca Toscana;
closed to the public.
Page 282.

Palazzo Pucci
Via dei Pucci, 6
Property of the Marchesi Pucci;
closed to the public.
Page 262.

Palazzo Ricasoli Firidolfi
Via Maggio, 7
Property of the Baroni Ricasoli;
closed to the public.
Page 232.

Palazzo Rosselli Del Turco
Borgo Santi Apostoli, 17
Property of the Conti Rosselli Del
Turco; closed to the public.
Page 238.

Palazzo Rucellai
Via della Vigna Nuova, 18
Property of the Marchesi Rucellai;
closed to the public.
Page 132.

Palazzo Strozzi
Piazza Strozzi, 1
Property of Istituto Nazionale
delle Assicurazioni (INA), an
insurance company; site of the
Gabinetto Scientifico Letterario
G.P. Vieusseux and the Istituto di
Studi sul Rinascimento, two
learned societies; the inner
courtyard is open to the public.
Page 106.

Palazzo Vecchio
Piazza della Signoria, 1
Property of the city of Florence;
open to the public.
Page 42.

Palazzo Venturi Ginori
Via della Scala, 85
Property of the Cassa di Risparmio
di Pisa; closed to the public.
Page 126.

Palazzo Ximenes da Sangallo
Borgo Pinti, 68
Property of the Princes Ruffo di
Calabria; closed to the public.
Page 156.

Index of names and places

The names of the palazzi featured in this volume appear in capital letters.